Skills Today

SQL Database Reporting

Simon Smart

Published by:

Simon Smart
4C Princess Towers
The Promenade
Port Erin, IOM,
Great Britain
IM1 5EP

Tel: +44 (0)845 458 3282 Fax: +44 (0)845 458 3281

E-mail: info@LearnDatabaseReporting.com
Web: LearnDatabaseReporting.com (this book's dedicated web site)

SECOND EDITION

International Standard Book Number (ISBN13): 978-1-9160586-6-8

1 2 4 6 8 10 9 7 5 4

Contents

Introduction

Almost every company in the world now relies on databases for their day to day operations, but they're often unable to extract the data they need from their databases. Reporting software can help but can't solve every problem. Every organization can benefit from a staff member who knows how to generate database reports using the SQL language, but SQL is a rare skill among most office staff.

Part of the reason that few people have SQL skills is that most related courses try to teach every aspect of database theory, including database design and server administration.

This course is different. It focuses entirely on database reporting and won't slow you down by trying to teach skills that you don't need. This course also focuses on skills that will be useful on many different types of database rather than teaching obscure commands that will only work on a certain type of database.

If you want to learn practical SQL reporting skills in the shortest time possible, this is the course for you.

How to use this course

This course works entirely with practical examples. To get the most out of the course you should follow each lesson's examples on your own computer.

To follow the course's examples, you will need a Windows computer with SQL Server Express installed. SQL Server Express can be downloaded for free and you will find full instructions on how to install it at the beginning of the course.

The SQL skills taught in this course are also applicable to other database products such as MySQL. You could theoretically complete this course using a different type of database but it's highly recommended that you use SQL Server Express.

The sample database used in this course can be downloaded for free from this course's official website at learndatabasereporting.com. Full instructions on how to install it are provided at the start of the course.

note

Databases that use the SQL language

The SQL language is used by many different database products, including:

Microsoft SQL Server

Microsoft Access

MySQL

PostgreSQL

SQLite

Lesson 1: Install SQL Server Express

The SQL language is used by a wide variety of database products (see sidebar). Database products tend to include special commands that are only used by that database engine, but outside of these commands the language works in the same way regardless of the database you are using.

This course is intended to be used with the free SQL Server Express, but the skills you will learn should be equally applicable to any database that uses the SQL language.

In this lesson you will download and install SQL Server Express.

1 Uninstall any existing copies of SQL Server.

It's possible for multiple instances of SQL Server to coexist on the same computer. This can cause confusion, so it is advisable to uninstall any copies of SQL Server that you already have installed.

2 Install SQL Server Express.

At the time this course was written, SQL Server 2017 Express could be downloaded from:

https://www.microsoft.com/en-us/sql-server/sql-server-editions-express

Since Microsoft could change their website at any time, it's possible that it will have been moved by the time you read this. In this case you should be able to find SQL Server Express by using a search engine.

1. Download SQL Server Express from Microsoft's website.

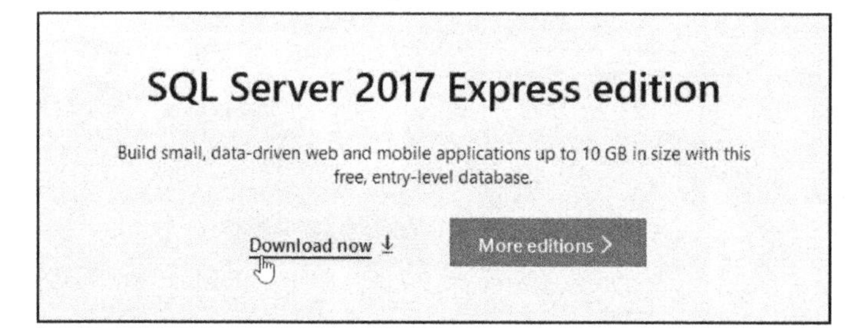

The download process may vary depending on your web browser. Most web browsers will automatically place downloaded files into your *Downloads* folder.

2. After downloading, open the installer.
3. Choose the *Basic* installation type.

note

Some versions of SQL Server include SSMS by default

At the time this book was written it was necessary to install SQL Server Management Studio (SSMS) separately, but this hasn't always been the case.

Some earlier versions of SQL Server automatically installed SSMS so you might want to check if you already have it installed.

note

Programs that connect to SQL databases

Databases are used by many different programs, including websites.

Many programs are used to create reports from SQL databases, including Microsoft Excel and Crystal Reports.

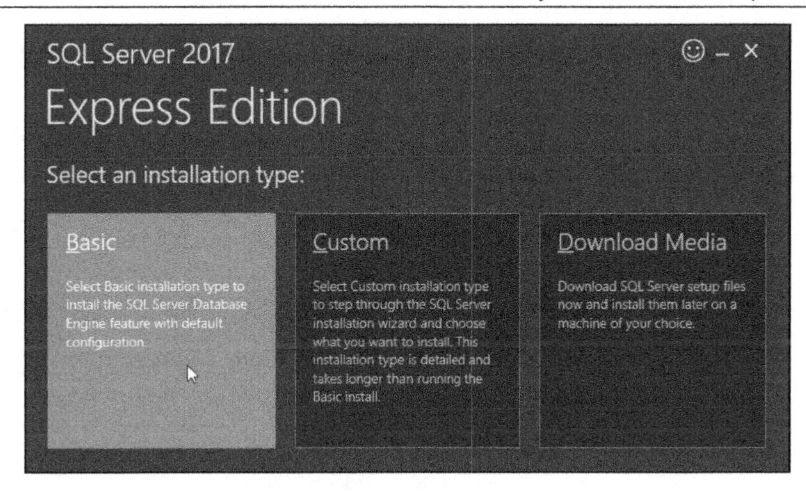

4. Click *Accept* to accept the terms and conditions.
5. Click *Install* to begin installation.

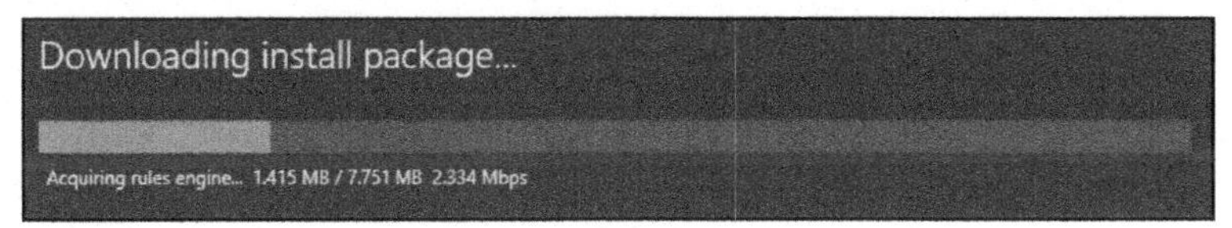

SQL server downloads and installs.

3 Install SQL Server Management Studio.

SQL server doesn't do anything until commands are sent to it. Many different pieces of software can connect to a SQL database (see sidebar), but Microsoft's free SQL Server Management Studio product is one of the best tools available for database administrators.

1. Click the *Install SSMS* button that appears after SQL Server installation finishes.

Your web browser opens and takes you to a page on Microsoft's website where you can download SQL Server Management Studio.

2. Click the download link and run the installer.

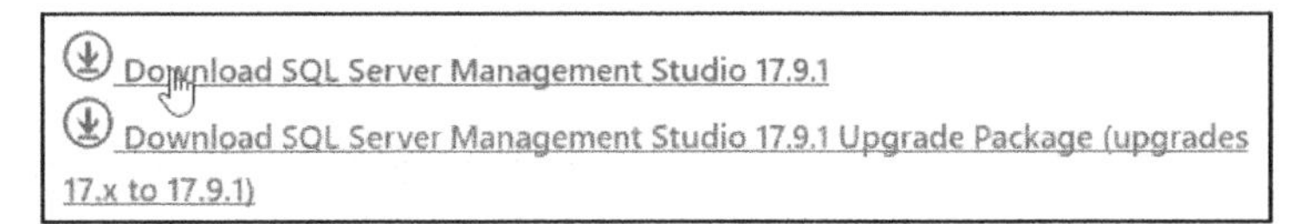

3. Click *Install* to install the program.

Lesson 2: Connect to SQL Server

Now that you have installed SQL Server Express it will automatically run in the background.

In this lesson you will use SQL Server Management Studio to connect to your SQL Server.

1 Open SQL Server Management Studio (SSMS).

SQL Server Management Studio opens and prompts you to enter the credentials needed to connect to a database.

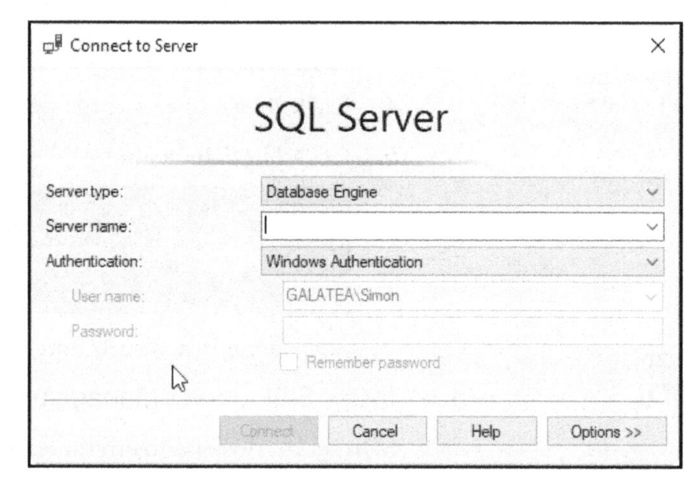

You can use SSMS to connect to any database, including databases on remote servers. In this case you are going to connect to the SQL Server Express database that you installed on your own computer.

2 Connect to your SQL Server Express database server.

1. Click the drop-down arrow next to *Server name* and click *<Browse for more…>*.

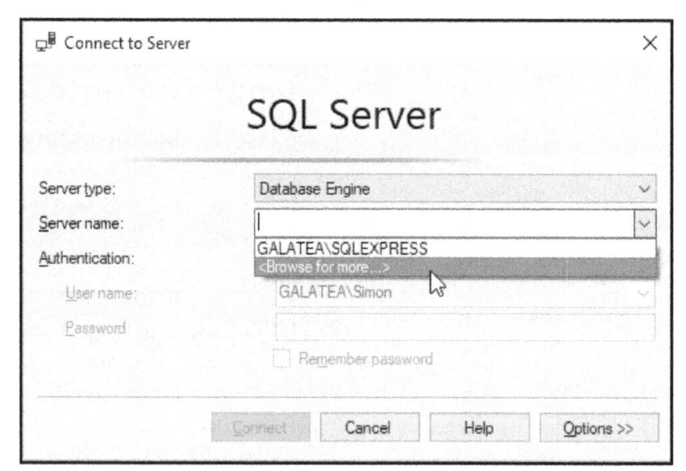

2. Click the + sign next to *Database Engine*.

   You should see a list of database instances installed on your computer.

   If SQL Server Express is the only copy of SQL Server on your computer, you will only see one item in the list with the name of your computer followed by *SQLEXPRESS*.

3. Click the *SQLEXPRESS* database and click *OK*.

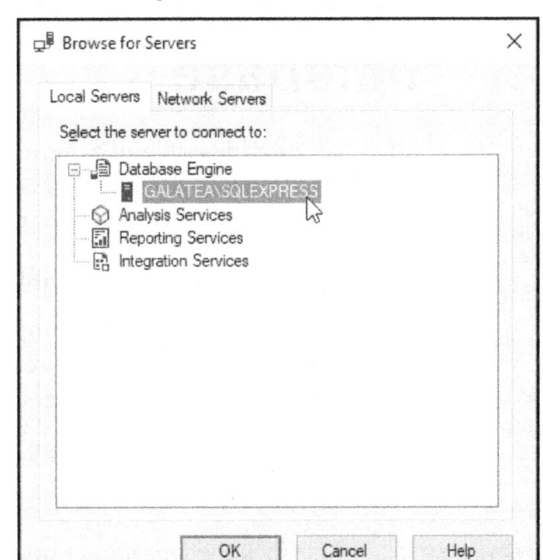

You should be returned to the previous dialog with the database name entered in the *Server name* box.

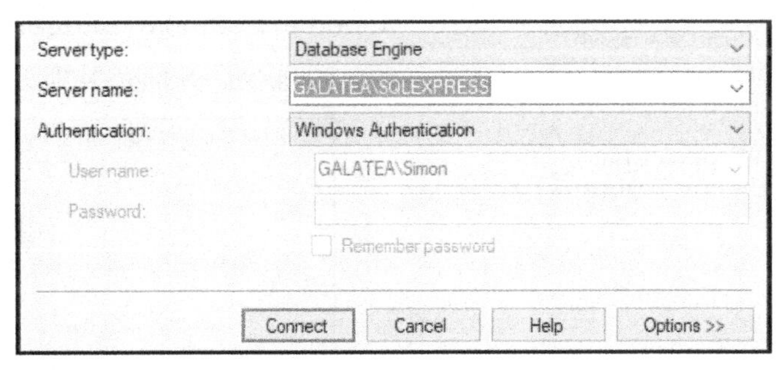

4. Click *Connect* to connect to the server.

   You have now connected to SQL Server. The *Object Explorer* pane on the left of the screen allows you to explore the databases on the server and configure security permissions.

   You can create a new SQL query by clicking the *New Query* button on the menu bar at the top of the screen.

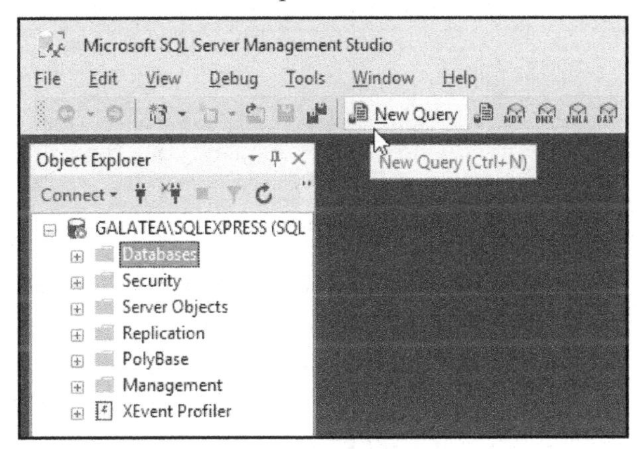

3 Keep SSMS open for the next lesson.

Lesson 3: Install the sample database

Microsoft provides several sample databases that you can use to practice. For this course you will use the *Northwind* sample database. In this lesson you will install the sample database by running a SQL script.

note

The sample database license

The sample databases are provided by Microsoft under the MIT license. This license allows the databases to be freely distributed and modified as long as the license is included.

You can find the full license included along with the sample databases.

tip

Keyboard shortcuts

Like most applications, SSMS offers keyboard shortcuts for many commands.

You can quickly open a file with the **<Ctrl>+<O>** keyboard shortcut.

1 Download the sample database script.

You can download the sample database script from this course's website or from Microsoft's website. The copy available from the website is identical to Microsoft's version.

1. Navigate to **learndatabasereporting.com**.
2. Click *Sample Databases* at the top of the screen.
3. Click the *Download* button to download the sample script.

2 Open SSMS and connect to SQL Server (if you haven't already done this).

3 Open the sample database script in SSMS.

1. Click *File→Open→File.*

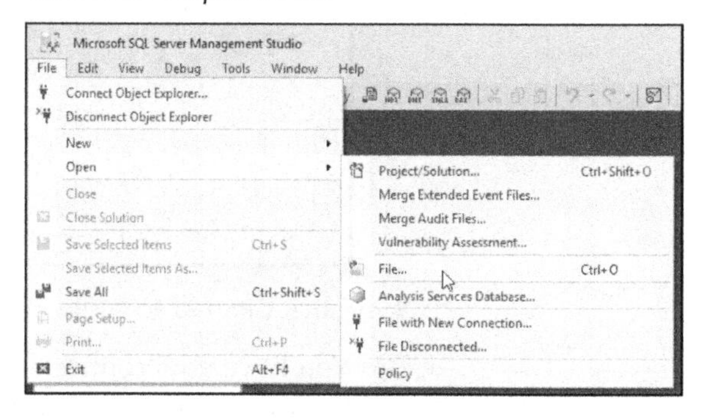

2. Navigate to the sample database script and click *Open*. The file name is *instnwnd.sql*.

The script opens in SSMS.

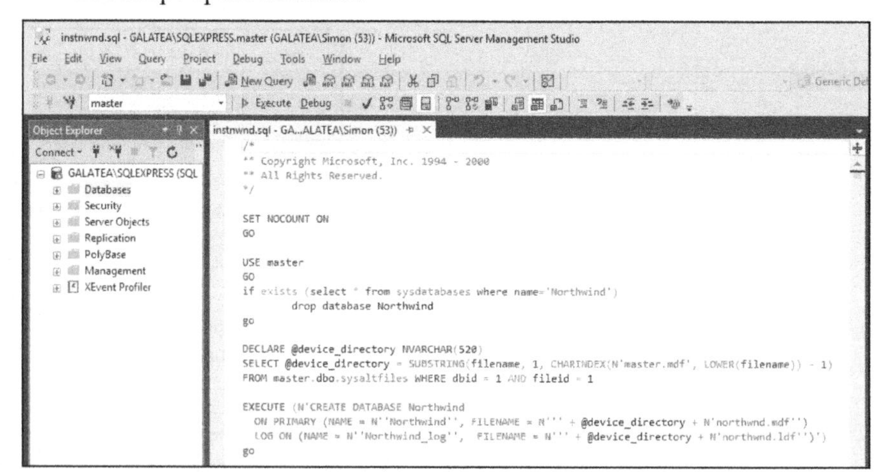

This is your first look at a SQL script. This is a complex script that creates database tables and data. As a database reporter your security permissions wouldn't usually allow you to run this kind of script, but you have full administrator's rights on your own copy of SQL Server.

There's no need to understand exactly how this script works. You just need to run it to install the test database.

4 Run the script to install the database.

Click the *Execute* button on the toolbar at the top of the screen.

It may take a few seconds for the script to run. After it has finished, a pane appears at the bottom of the screen, hopefully informing you that the commands were completed successfully (see sidebar if an error message appears).

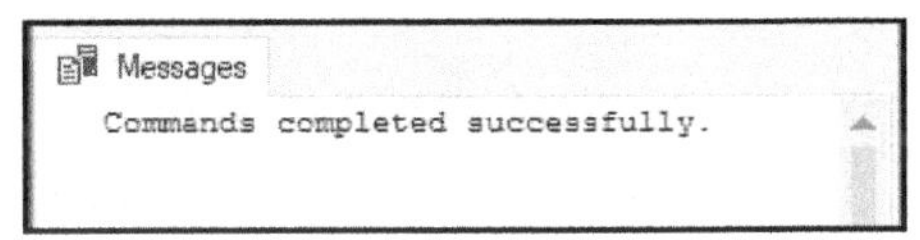

This is the area where the results of your queries are displayed.

5 Check that the database has been installed.

The new database won't immediately appear in the SSMS interface. You'll have to tell it to refresh first.

1. Right click on the *Databases* folder in the left pane and click *Refresh* from the shortcut menu.

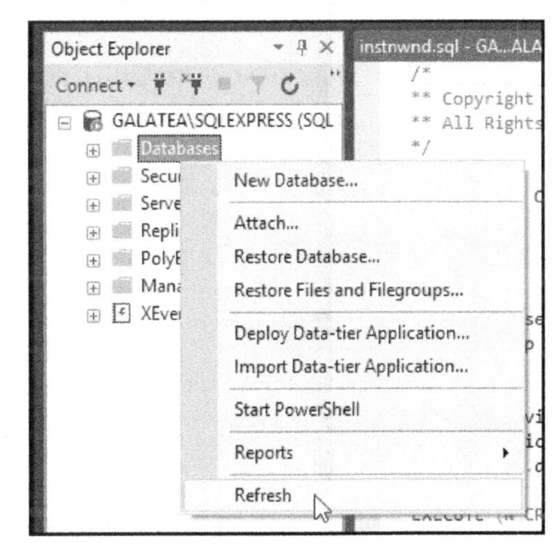

2. Click the + icon next to *Databases*.

   You should now see the *Northwind* database in the list.

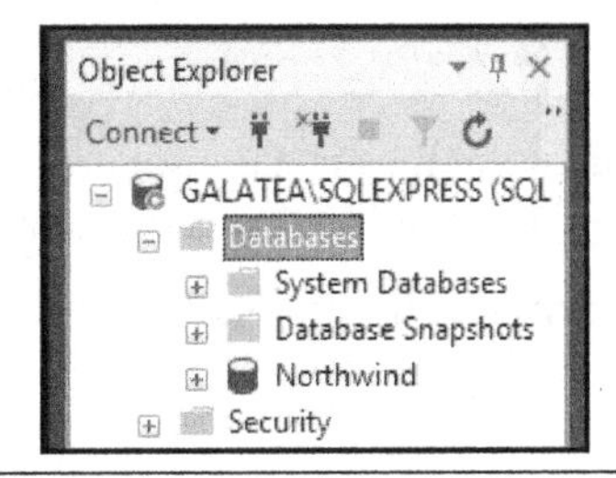

note

If an error message appears

There are two main reasons why an error message may appear when you run the database script:

1. You may have a very old version of SQL Server installed.

If you think this may be the case, return to the previous lesson and make sure that the correct version is installed.

2. You may already have a copy of the Northwind database installed.

The script may fail if there is already a database called *Northwind*. If you want to remove the old copy and replace it with a new one you can delete the existing *Northwind* database by right-clicking on it and clicking *Delete* from the shortcut menu.

tip

Keyboard shortcuts

You can quickly execute a query by pressing the the **<F5>** key.

note

What is a relational database?

Any form of information storage can be said to be a database, but most databases in the world of commerce are *relational* databases.

Relational databases contain multiple tables of data that are joined together with 'relationships'.

By using multiple tables, relational databases avoid repeating the same data more than once, making them more efficient than, for example, an Excel spreadsheet.

You'll learn much more about how relational databases work later in this course, in: *Lesson 20: Understand relationships*.

Lesson 4: Explore a database

You need to know how a database is structured before you can begin to query it. Fortunately, SSMS makes it easy to examine a database's structure.

1 Open SSMS and connect to your SQL Server (if you haven't already done this).

2 Examine the tables in the database.

1. Expand the *Databases* folder in the *Object Explorer* pane by clicking the + sign to the left of it.

   You should see the *Northwind* database, just as you did in the previous lesson.

2. Expand the *Northwind* database.

   You should see several subfolders that contain different objects within the *Northwind* database.

3. Expand the *Tables* subfolder.

   You can now see all of the tables within the *Northwind* database (the items with the ▦ icon).

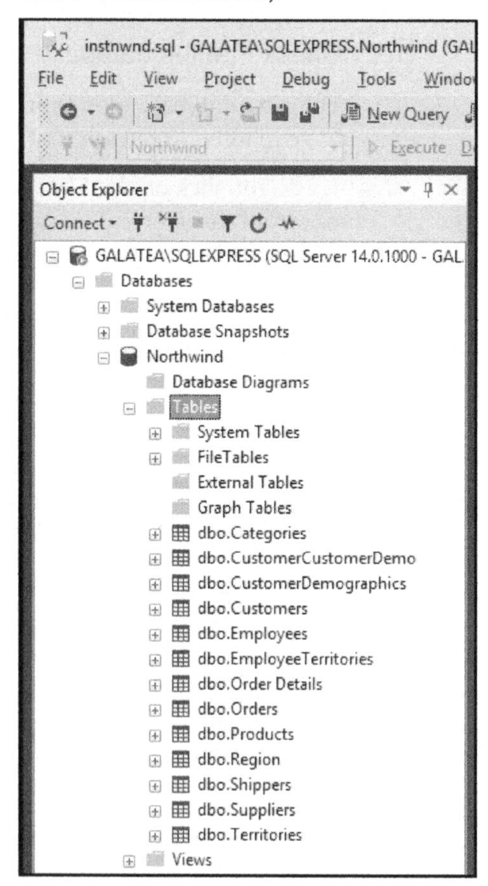

Most databases have several tables that contain the actual data. As you can see, the *Northwind* database has 13 tables.

3 Examine the contents of the *Customers* table.

As well as viewing the names of the tables in the database, SSMS also allows you to quickly view a snapshot of their contents. This can be very helpful to establish the types of data that a table contains.

Right click the *Customers* table and click *Select Top 1000 Rows* from the shortcut menu.

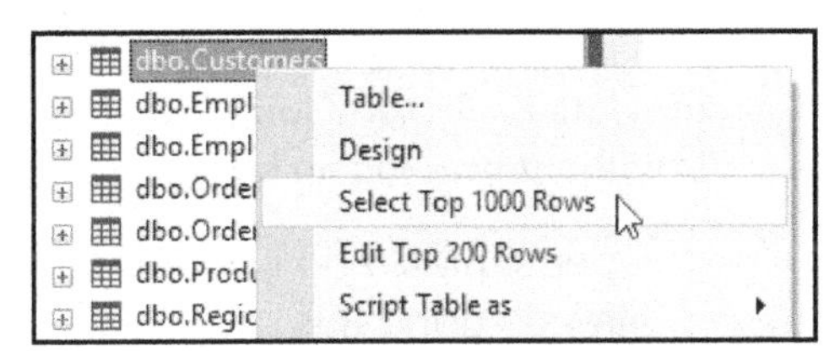

SSMS automatically generates and runs a SQL script that displays the top 1000 rows in the *Customers* table. You should see the script in the central pane of the SSMS interface and the query results in the bottom pane.

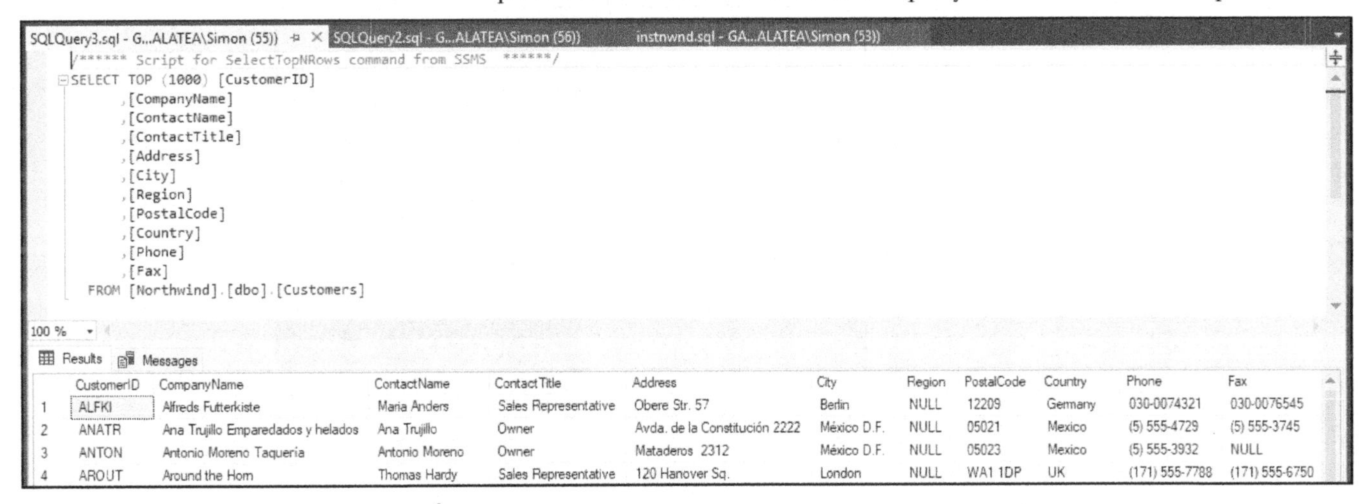

4 Examine the design of the *Customers* table.

Right click the *Customers* table and click *Design* from the shortcut menu.

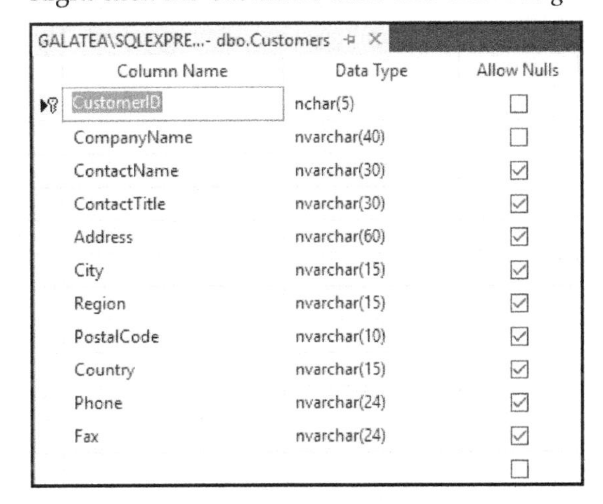

You can now see the design of the *Customers* table. Database designers and administrators use this interface to design and modify tables, but for reporting purposes you're only interested in the *Data Type* and *Allow Nulls* columns. You'll work with data types and nulls in depth in: *Lesson 16: Work with NULL values and the IN keyword.*

Lesson 5: Write your first database query

Many other courses try to extensively teach you about relational database theory before writing any queries. This course is more practical. You'll learn about relationships and joins later in the course, but you can learn a lot of useful skills without needing an in-depth knowledge of relational database theory.

1. Open SSMS and connect to your SQL Server (if you haven't already done this).

2. Create a new query.

   Click the *New Query* button on the top toolbar.

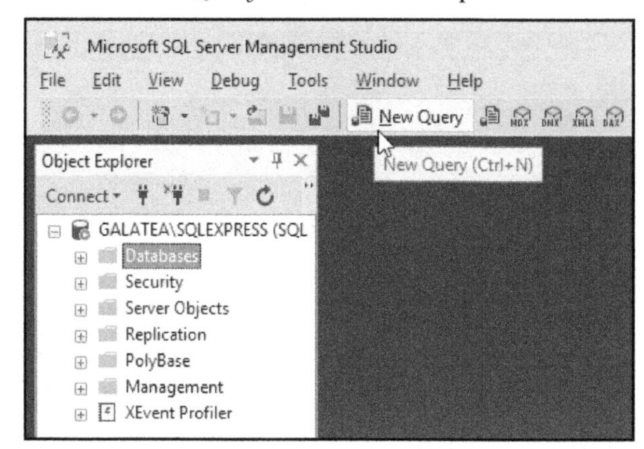

   An empty window appears in the central pane of the interface, ready for you to enter a query.

3. Select the correct database to query.

   The drop-down menu on the top toolbar allows you to select which database should be queried. This usually defaults to the *master* database, which is used by SQL Server's subsystems to store information about the server and its contents.

   Click the drop-down menu and select the *Northwind* database.

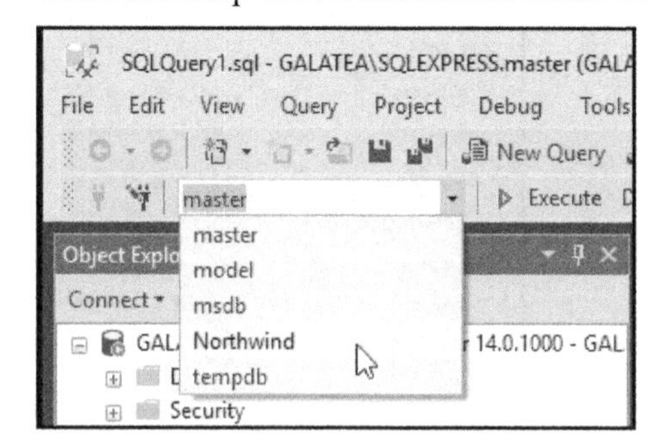

   It isn't strictly necessary to do this, but it ensures that your queries will default to the correct database.

4. Write a query to display the contents of the *Orders* table.

   Type the following query into the empty query pane:

note

The USE statement

As an alternative to using the drop-down menu or the fully qualified database name, you can also use the *USE* statement.

To make your SQL code default to the Northwind database you can place the following line at the beginning:

```
USE Northwind
```

The scripts in this course will assume that you have selected the correct database from the drop-down menu, but the *USE* statement can be useful when writing scripts that need to be used on a different database server.

```
SELECT *
FROM [Northwind].[dbo].[Orders]
```

This is your first SQL query.

The SELECT command tells the database that you want to extract and display data. It will be the first command in almost all database reports.

The asterisk (*) tells the database that you want it to display everything in the table. You'll replace this with more specific instructions later.

The FROM command tells the database where you want it to look for the data. In this case you want the *Orders* table in the *Northwind* database. *dbo* is the *schema* that the *Orders* table belongs to. Most databases only use the default *dbo* (database owner) schema, but some use multiple schemas to group tables together.

Since you selected the database using the drop-down menu, it isn't actually necessary to write the full path to the table. The square brackets are also unnecessary unless the table or database name contains spaces. You can shorten the query considerably to:

```
SELECT *
FROM Orders
```

A query like this takes very slightly longer to execute because the database needs to figure out the correct schema each time it runs.

I prefer to use the shorter, more concise style for one-time queries and testing purposes, but it's best practice to use the full table path.

The queries shown in this course will generally use the full path to the database, but some of the more complex queries will use the shorter form to make them easier to understand.

note

SQL commands are not case sensitive

SQL commands are almost always written in all caps, such as you can see here with the SELECT and FROM commands, but it isn't actually necessary to do this.

The following query will work without any problems:

```
select *
from Orders
```

Commands such as SELECT and FROM are often known as 'statements' and they can span several lines. The all-caps convention helps you to see where statements begin and end, as well as making your code more readable for other users who are familiar with this convention.

note

Table names can be case sensitive

Table names are not case sensitive by default, but this can be changed in the database settings.

It's best practice to always use the correct casing for table names.

5 Execute the query.

Click the *Execute* button on the top toolbar.

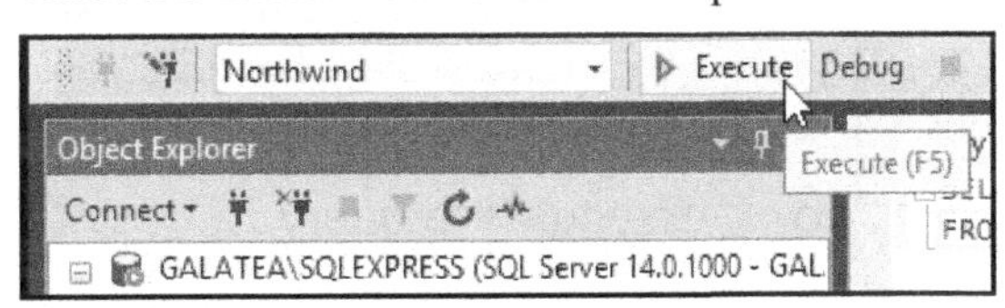

The query runs and the results are displayed in a pane at the bottom of the screen.

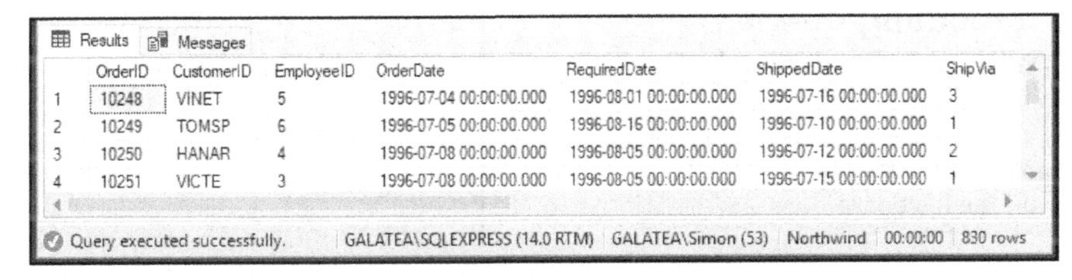

	OrderID	CustomerID	EmployeeID	OrderDate	RequiredDate	ShippedDate	ShipVia
1	10248	VINET	5	1996-07-04 00:00:00.000	1996-08-01 00:00:00.000	1996-07-16 00:00:00.000	3
2	10249	TOMSP	6	1996-07-05 00:00:00.000	1996-08-16 00:00:00.000	1996-07-10 00:00:00.000	1
3	10250	HANAR	4	1996-07-08 00:00:00.000	1996-08-05 00:00:00.000	1996-07-12 00:00:00.000	2
4	10251	VICTE	3	1996-07-08 00:00:00.000	1996-08-05 00:00:00.000	1996-07-15 00:00:00.000	1

Notice that the yellow bar at the bottom of the pane shows you that the query returned 830 rows of data. You can use the scrollbars to examine the entire contents of the *Orders* table.

Lesson 6: Understand the SELECT statement and save a query

All database reports that extract and display data contain the SELECT statement. You'll write your first query using SELECT in this lesson and will see how to save your query to a file.

1 Open SSMS and connect to your SQL Server (if you haven't already done this).

2 Write a query to display a list of company names from the *Suppliers* table.

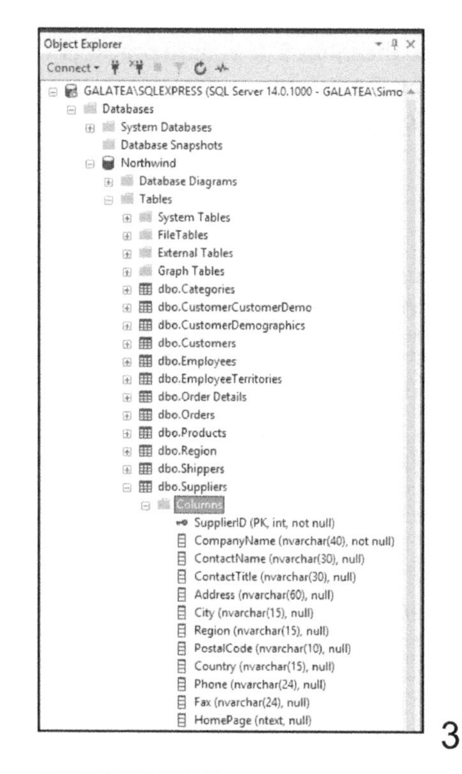

This step is intentionally a little vague; it's the kind of request you might get as a database analyst. You'll need to examine the *Suppliers* table to figure out which column contains the data you need.

1. Expand the *Northwind* database in the left pane.
2. Expand the *Tables* folder.
3. Expand the *Suppliers* table.
4. Expand the *Columns* folder to display a list of columns in the table.

   You can see that the data you need is in the *CompanyName* column. You could also have checked the columns in the table by viewing the table's contents as you did in the previous lesson.

5. Type the following query:

```
SELECT CompanyName
FROM Northwind.dbo.Suppliers
```

In the previous lesson you used the asterisk (*) to return everything from a table. This time you're telling the database that you only want the *CompanyName* column.

3 Execute the query.

All 29 of the company names are returned from the *Suppliers* table.

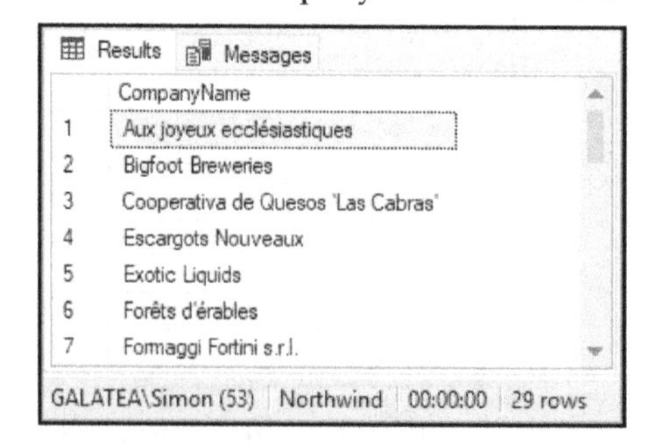

tip

Executing queries with the keyboard

You can quickly execute a query by pressing the <F5> key on the keyboard.

4 Write a query to display the company names, contact names and addresses from the *Suppliers* table.

This time you're going to write a query to return 3 columns from the table.

note

Why is *Address* highlighted?

You might notice that the word *Address* is highlighted in blue when writing this query. This is happening because SQL Server considers the word *Address* to be reserved for a different purpose.

In this case the word *Address* won't cause any problems, but reserved names can cause errors in some cases. If this happens you can fix the problem by enclosing the name in square brackets: *[Address]*.

You also need to use square brackets to refer to names that contain spaces.

A well-designed database avoids the need for square brackets by avoiding reserved names and spaces, but some analysts prefer to use square brackets at all times to avoid any potential problems.

This course will only use square brackets when necessary, to make it clear when they are and are not needed.

tip

Saving with the keyboard

You can quickly save a query with the **<Ctrl>+<S>** keyboard shortcut.

Modify your query to:

```
SELECT CompanyName, ContactName, Address
FROM Northwind.dbo.Suppliers
```

You can enter as many columns as you need in the SELECT statement, separated by commas.

Line breaks are ignored by SQL queries so you can use them to make your queries more readable. Some analysts might find this query more readable written this way:

```
SELECT
CompanyName,
ContactName,
Address
FROM Northwind.dbo.Suppliers
```

Line breaks aren't really needed in this query, but they're very helpful with larger SELECT statements.

Using line breaks and spaces can make your queries much easier to read and understand. You can also indent lines by using the **<Tab>** key.

5 Save the query as: **SupplierData.sql**

1. Click: *File*→Save *SQLQuery1.sql As.*

   The file name may be slightly different (such as *SQLQuery5.sql*), depending on how many new queries you have created since opening SSMS.

2. Enter **SupplierData.sql** into the *File name* box, choose a location to save to and click *Save.*

Your query is now saved and can be reopened later in the same way as you opened the sample database script in: *Lesson 3: Install the sample database.*

SQL queries are plain text, so you can also copy your scripts into any text document and paste them back into SSMS later if you prefer.

You'll discover how to save SQL queries onto the server itself later in the course, in: *Lesson 29: Create a View.*

Lesson 7: Sort with ORDER BY and export query results

In this lesson you'll learn how to sort the results of queries and how to export query results as files that can be sent to other users.

1 Open SSMS and connect to your SQL Server (if you haven't already done this).

2 Write a query to extract all records from the *Orders* table.

You saw how to do this in *Lesson 5: Write your first database query*. The query should be:

```
SELECT *
FROM Northwind.dbo.Orders
```

3 Execute the query.

All records in the *Orders* table are displayed. Notice that they are not shown in any particular order.

Results | Messages

	OrderID	CustomerID	EmployeeID	OrderDate	RequiredDate
1	10248	VINET	5	1996-07-04 00:00:00.000	1996-08-01 00:00:00.000
2	10249	TOMSP	6	1996-07-05 00:00:00.000	1996-08-16 00:00:00.000
3	10250	HANAR	4	1996-07-08 00:00:00.000	1996-08-05 00:00:00.000
4	10251	VICTE	3	1996-07-08 00:00:00.000	1996-08-05 00:00:00.000
5	10252	SUPRD	4	1996-07-09 00:00:00.000	1996-08-06 00:00:00.000

4 Modify the query to sort the results by *CustomerID*.

The ORDER BY statement lets you sort your query results.

SQL statements must be written in the correct order. ORDER BY must be placed after the SELECT and FROM statements.

Add an ORDER BY statement to the query as shown:

```
SELECT *
FROM Northwind.dbo.Orders
ORDER BY CustomerID
```

5 Execute the query.

The results are now sorted by *CustomerID*, in ascending alphabetical order. This is the default sort order.

Results | Messages

	OrderID	CustomerID	EmployeeID	OrderDate	RequiredDate
1	10643	ALFKI	6	1997-08-25 00:00:00.000	1997-09-22 00:00:00.000
2	10692	ALFKI	4	1997-10-03 00:00:00.000	1997-10-31 00:00:00.000
3	10702	ALFKI	4	1997-10-13 00:00:00.000	1997-11-24 00:00:00.000
4	10835	ALFKI	1	1998-01-15 00:00:00.000	1998-02-12 00:00:00.000
5	10952	ALFKI	1	1998-03-16 00:00:00.000	1998-04-27 00:00:00.000

6 Modify the query to sort by first by *CustomerID* and then by *OrderDate*.

The results are sorted by customer ID, but they are shown in no particular date order. Modify the query as follows:

note

The order of statements

SQL statements have to be written in a specific order. SELECT usually comes first, followed by FROM.

You haven't seen every statement available yet, but here is the order that they should be written:

```
USE
SELECT
FROM
WHERE
GROUP BY
HAVING
ORDER BY
```

note

Default sorting

If you don't supply an *ORDER BY* statement, the query results generally show the records in the order in which they were added to the database.

It's possible for records to be updated, deleted and replaced at any time so you shouldn't rely on this to show records in order of date.

note

CSV files

CSV stands for "Comma Separated Values". A CSV file contains data separated by commas. For example:

```
11011,ALFKI,3,
1998-04-09,1998-05-07
```

CSV files can be opened by Microsoft Excel and can be opened and imported by many other programs.

note

Syntactic sugar

The SQL language often allows commands to be entered in multiple ways, usually offering a more verbose alternative that is intended to make your code easier to read. This is known as "syntactic sugar".

In this lesson you use the *ASC* and *DESC* keywords to control sort order, but they can also be written as *ASCENDING* and *DESCENDING* to make their purpose clearer.

This course generally uses the shorter forms of commands.

note

Copying and pasting

As well as saving the query results as a file, you can also copy results directly from the *Results* pane and paste them into another program, usually an Excel spreadsheet. This is often the quickest way to extract the results of a query.

You can copy query results by selecting them in the *Results* pane and clicking *Edit→Copy* or using the **<Ctrl>+<C>** keyboard shortcut.

```
SELECT *
FROM Northwind.dbo.Orders
ORDER BY CustomerID, OrderDate
```

Just like the SELECT statement, you can sort by as many columns as you need by separating them with commas. The order of the columns is important. This ORDER BY statement will first sort the results by *CustomerID* and then by *OrderDate*.

7 Execute the query.

The results are now sorted by customer ID and order date, both in ascending order.

Results | Messages

	OrderID	CustomerID	EmployeeID	OrderDate	RequiredDate
1	10643	ALFKI	6	1997-08-25 00:00:00.000	1997-09-22 00:00:00.000
2	10692	ALFKI	4	1997-10-03 00:00:00.000	1997-10-31 00:00:00.000
3	10702	ALFKI	4	1997-10-13 00:00:00.000	1997-11-24 00:00:00.000
4	10835	ALFKI	1	1998-01-15 00:00:00.000	1998-02-12 00:00:00.000
5	10952	ALFKI	1	1998-03-16 00:00:00.000	1998-04-27 00:00:00.000

8 Modify the query to sort the dates in descending order (most recent first).

ORDER BY allows you to use the keywords *ASCENDING* and *DESCENDING* to control the sort order. You can shorten these to *ASC* and *DESC*. Modify the query to:

```
SELECT *
FROM Northwind.dbo.Orders
ORDER BY CustomerID, OrderDate DESC
```

9 Execute the query.

The results are now sorted by *CustomerID* in ascending order and by *OrderDate* in descending order.

Results | Messages

	OrderID	CustomerID	EmployeeID	OrderDate	RequiredDate
1	11011	ALFKI	3	1998-04-09 00:00:00.000	1998-05-07 00:00:00.000
2	10952	ALFKI	1	1998-03-16 00:00:00.000	1998-04-27 00:00:00.000
3	10835	ALFKI	1	1998-01-15 00:00:00.000	1998-02-12 00:00:00.000
4	10702	ALFKI	4	1997-10-13 00:00:00.000	1997-11-24 00:00:00.000
5	10692	ALFKI	4	1997-10-03 00:00:00.000	1997-10-31 00:00:00.000

10 Export the query results as a CSV file.

You can export the results of a query as a file, making it easy to distribute query results.

1. Right click in the query results and click *Save Results As* from the shortcut menu.
2. Save the results as: **SortedOrders.csv**

The query results are saved as a CSV file, which can be opened in Microsoft Excel and many other programs.

note

Spaces in table names are bad design

It's generally considered best practice to avoid spaces in table names, but you'll almost certainly encounter design mistakes in databases that you work on.

It's useful to know how to work around these issues, so it's helpful that there are some mistakes in Microsoft's sample database!

Lesson 8: Use the TOP and DISTINCT keywords

The TOP keyword lets you limit your queries to display a certain number of records, while the DISTINCT keyword is used to extract unique values from a list containing duplicate entries.

1 Open SSMS and connect to your SQL Server (if you haven't already done this).

2 Write a query to extract all records from the *Order Details* table.

The *Order Details* table has a space in its name. If you think back to *Lesson 5: Write your first database query*, you'll remember that names containing spaces must be enclosed in square brackets.

The query should look like this:

```
SELECT *
FROM Northwind.dbo.[Order Details]
```

If you try running this query without the square brackets you will see an error message.

3 Modify the query to display the top 10 sales by quantity.

You cannot use the TOP keyword without an ORDER BY statement. To retrieve the 10 sales that had the highest quantity, use the query:

```
SELECT TOP 10 *
FROM Northwind.dbo.[Order Details]
ORDER BY Quantity DESC
```

It's important that the query results are sorted in descending (*DESC*) order so that the highest quantities are shown first. Without the *DESC* keyword the 10 orders with the lowest quantities would be shown first instead, because *ORDER BY* defaults to sorting in ascending order.

4 Execute the query.

The top 10 sales with the highest quantity are shown.

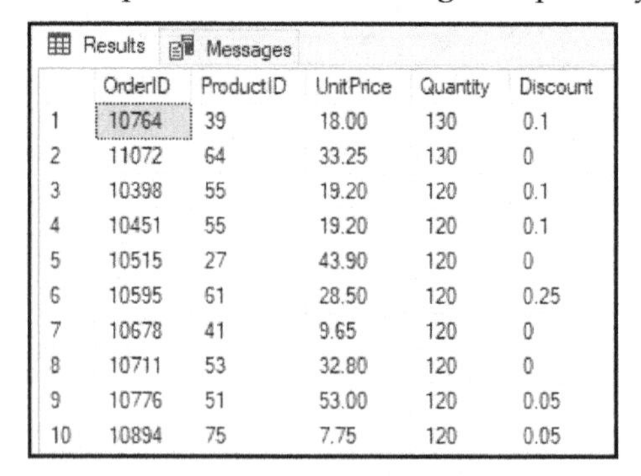

Results | Messages

	OrderID	ProductID	UnitPrice	Quantity	Discount
1	10764	39	18.00	130	0.1
2	11072	64	33.25	130	0
3	10398	55	19.20	120	0.1
4	10451	55	19.20	120	0.1
5	10515	27	43.90	120	0
6	10595	61	28.50	120	0.25
7	10678	41	9.65	120	0
8	10711	53	32.80	120	0
9	10776	51	53.00	120	0.05
10	10894	75	7.75	120	0.05

5 Modify the query to display the top 25 percent of orders.

You can specify a percentage as well as a specific number of rows for the TOP keyword to return. Modify the query to:

```
SELECT TOP 25 PERCENT *
FROM Northwind.dbo.[Order Details]
ORDER BY Quantity DESC
```

6 Execute the query.

25% of the records in the *Order Details* table are shown, sorted by *Quantity*.

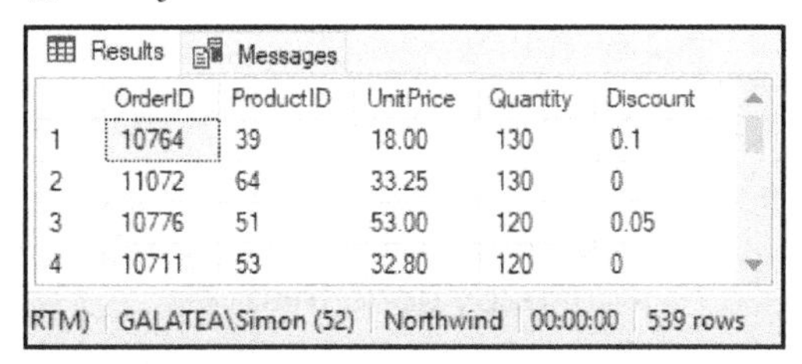

	OrderID	ProductID	UnitPrice	Quantity	Discount
1	10764	39	18.00	130	0.1
2	11072	64	33.25	130	0
3	10776	51	53.00	120	0.05
4	10711	53	32.80	120	0

7 Write a query to extract a unique list of product IDs that have been sold.

1. Execute the following query:

```
SELECT ProductID
FROM Northwind.dbo.[Order Details]
```

The query returns the *ProductID* values from every record in the *Order Details* table.

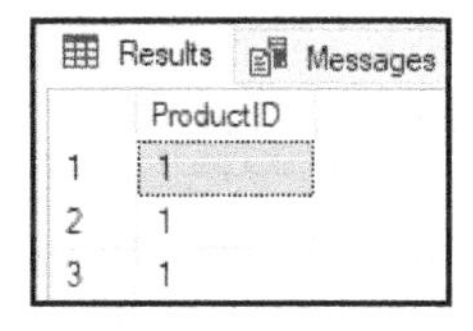

	ProductID
1	1
2	1
3	1

You can see every *ProductID* that has been sold but you're seeing separate records for each sale, which isn't really what you wanted. The *DISTINCT* keyword will instruct the query to only return unique values.

2. Modify the query to:

```
SELECT DISTINCT ProductID
FROM Northwind.dbo.[Order Details]
```

3. Execute the query.

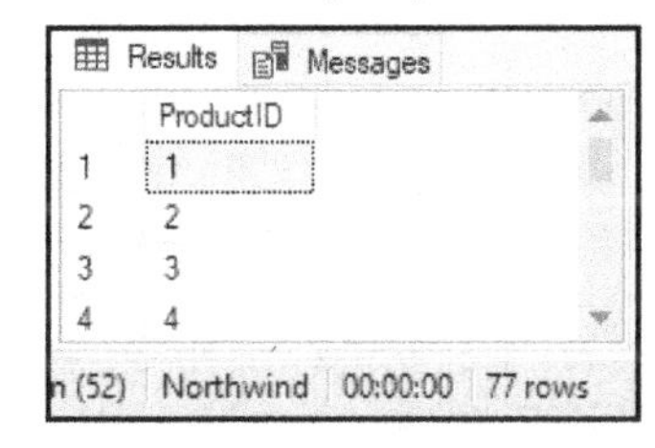

	ProductID
1	1
2	2
3	3
4	4

A unique list of product IDs is shown. You can see the IDs of all 77 products that have been sold.

note

DISTINCT works with all columns in the query

The DISTINCT keyword can be used with a SELECT statement that contains multiple columns.

If you use the DISTINCT keyword the query will omit any records where all columns are duplicated.

For example, to return a unique list of product IDs and the prices that they have been sold at, you could use the query:

```
SELECT DISTINCT
ProductID, UnitPrice
```

Lesson 9: Filter results with WHERE

So far, your queries have mostly worked with every record in a table, the exception being the ones that used the TOP keyword to limit the number of results returned.

The WHERE keyword is used to filter your query results and is often the most complex part of a query. The WHERE statement comes after the FROM statement.

1. Open SSMS and connect to your SQL Server (if you haven't already done this).

2. Write a query to extract all records from the *Orders* table.

```
SELECT *
FROM Northwind.dbo.Orders
```

3. Modify the query to only show orders made by *EmployeeID* 5.

   The WHERE statement lets you add filtering rules to a query. Modify the query to:

```
SELECT *
FROM Northwind.dbo.Orders
WHERE EmployeeID=5
```

   This tells the database that you only want to see orders for EmployeeID 5.

4. Execute the query.

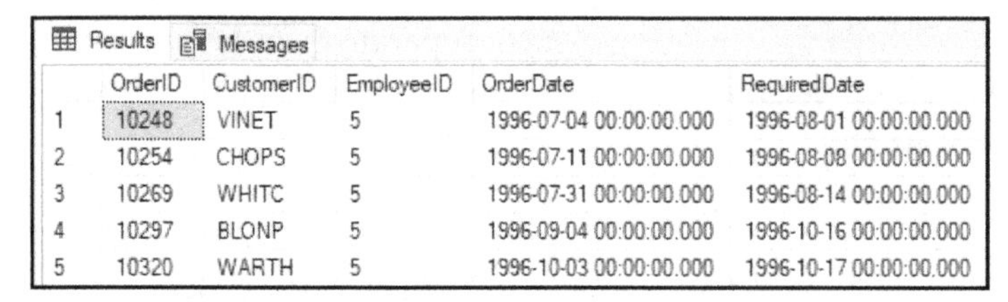

	OrderID	CustomerID	EmployeeID	OrderDate	RequiredDate
1	10248	VINET	5	1996-07-04 00:00:00.000	1996-08-01 00:00:00.000
2	10254	CHOPS	5	1996-07-11 00:00:00.000	1996-08-08 00:00:00.000
3	10269	WHITC	5	1996-07-31 00:00:00.000	1996-08-14 00:00:00.000
4	10297	BLONP	5	1996-09-04 00:00:00.000	1996-10-16 00:00:00.000
5	10320	WARTH	5	1996-10-03 00:00:00.000	1996-10-17 00:00:00.000

   All orders for EmployeeID 5 are displayed.

5. Modify the query to only show orders made to *CustomerID* 'VINET'.

   To specify a textual value in SQL code, you need to enclose it in single quotes. The query should be:

```
SELECT *
FROM Northwind.dbo.Orders
WHERE CustomerID='VINET'
```

   The word *VINET* is highlighted in red, but that doesn't mean you've made a mistake. The red highlight is how SSMS color codes textual values for clarity.

6. Execute the query.

   The 5 orders made to the CustomerID *VINET* are shown:

Results | Messages

	OrderID	CustomerID	EmployeeID	OrderDate	RequiredDate
1	10248	VINET	5	1996-07-04 00:00:00.000	1996-08-01 00:00:00.000
2	10274	VINET	6	1996-08-06 00:00:00.000	1996-09-03 00:00:00.000
3	10295	VINET	2	1996-09-02 00:00:00.000	1996-09-30 00:00:00.000
4	10737	VINET	2	1997-11-11 00:00:00.000	1997-12-09 00:00:00.000
5	10739	VINET	3	1997-11-12 00:00:00.000	1997-12-10 00:00:00.000

7 Modify the query to show orders with a *Freight* value greater than or equal to 500.

You can use the greater than (>) and less than (<) symbols in the WHERE statement, as well as other mathematical operators. You'll cover mathematical operators in more depth in: *Lesson 11: Use simple mathematical operators and custom column names.*

Modify the query to:

```
SELECT *
FROM Northwind.dbo.Orders
WHERE Freight >= 500
```

8 Execute the query.

The 13 orders with a freight value of 500 or more are shown:

Results | Messages

	OrderID	CustomerID	EmployeeID	OrderDate	RequiredDate
1	10372	QUEEN	5	1996-12-04 00:00:00.000	1997-01-01 00:00:00.000
2	10479	RATTC	3	1997-03-19 00:00:00.000	1997-04-16 00:00:00.000
3	10514	ERNSH	3	1997-04-22 00:00:00.000	1997-05-20 00:00:00.000
4	10540	QUICK	3	1997-05-19 00:00:00.000	1997-06-16 00:00:00.000
5	10612	SAVEA	1	1997-07-28 00:00:00.000	1997-08-25 00:00:00.000

9 Modify the query to show orders with an *OrderDate* on or later than the 1st of January 1998.

SQL code allows dates to be entered in several different ways (see sidebar).

Modify the query to:

```
SELECT *
FROM Northwind.dbo.Orders
WHERE OrderDate >= '01 Jan 1998'
```

You will cover more advanced date filtering later in the course.

10 Execute the query.

All sales on or after the 1st of January 1998 are displayed.

Results | Messages

	OrderID	CustomerID	EmployeeID	OrderDate	RequiredDate
1	10808	OLDWO	2	1998-01-01 00:00:00.000	1998-01-29 00:00:00.000
2	10809	WELLI	7	1998-01-01 00:00:00.000	1998-01-29 00:00:00.000
3	10810	LAUGB	2	1998-01-01 00:00:00.000	1998-01-29 00:00:00.000
4	10811	LINOD	8	1998-01-02 00:00:00.000	1998-01-30 00:00:00.000
5	10812	REGGC	5	1998-01-02 00:00:00.000	1998-01-30 00:00:00.000

note

Different ways to enter dates

SQL Server stores dates in the format Year/Month/Day. It will recognize dates in several different formats, but it's advisable to use the format shown in this lesson to avoid any ambiguity.

The following are all valid ways to enter the date:

```
'01 Jan 1998'
'01 January 1998'
'1998/Jan/01'
'1998-01-01'
'1998/01/01'
```

Lesson 10: Use the LIKE keyword for inexact filters

Sometimes you don't want to filter for exact values and instead want to perform a 'fuzzy' search. The LIKE keyword enables you to do this.

1 Open SSMS and connect to your SQL Server (if you haven't already done this).

2 Execute a query to extract all records from the *Products* table.

This is a simple query:

```
SELECT *
FROM Northwind.dbo.Products
```

If you examine the *QuantityPerUnit* column in the query results you can see that products are provided in boxes, bags, bottles, etc. and that this information is stored as text.

	ProductID	ProductName	SupplierID	CategoryID	QuantityPerUnit
1	1	Chai	1	1	10 boxes x 20 bags
2	2	Chang	1	1	24 - 12 oz bottles
3	3	Aniseed Syrup	1	2	12 - 550 ml bottles
4	4	Chef Anton's Cajun Seasoning	2	2	48 - 6 oz jars
5	5	Chef Anton's Gumbo Mix	2	2	36 boxes

3 Modify the query to only display products that are provided in *bottles*.

The text in the *QuantityPerUnit* column is different in each column so you couldn't use a simple filter like the one you used in the previous lesson.

To perform this kind of search you will need to use the *LIKE* keyword in place of the = sign. The LIKE keyword allows you to use wildcard symbols, and the % symbol is the wildcard that you will use most of the time.

Alter the query to:

```
SELECT *
FROM Northwind.dbo.Products
WHERE QuantityPerUnit LIKE '%bottles%'
```

This tells the server that you want to see records that contain the text *bottles*, with anything before or after it. The % wildcards will match any number of characters or no text at all.

The products that are provided in bottles are extracted and displayed.

	ProductID	ProductName	SupplierID	CategoryID	QuantityPerUnit
1	2	Chang	1	1	24 - 12 oz bottles
2	3	Aniseed Syrup	1	2	12 - 550 ml bottles
3	15	Genen Shouyu	6	2	24 - 250 ml bottles
4	34	Sasquatch Ale	16	1	24 - 12 oz bottles
5	35	Steeleye Stout	16	1	24 - 12 oz bottles

note

Searching for % and _ symbols

There may be times when you actually want to search for a % or _ symbol rather than allowing them to be used as wildcards. You can do this by enclosing the symbols in square brackets.

For example, you can search for values ending in 100% by using:

```
LIKE '%100[%]'
```

4 Execute a query to display all records from the *Customers* table.

This is another simple query.

```
SELECT *
FROM Northwind.dbo.Customers
```

Notice the 5 letter ID codes in the *CustomerID* column. Imagine that your shipping department finds a damaged label and only the second and fourth letters in the code are legible.

	CustomerID	CompanyName	ContactName
1	ALFKI	Alfreds Futterkiste	Maria Anders
2	ANATR	Ana Trujillo Emparedados y helados	Ana Trujillo
3	ANTON	Antonio Moreno Taquería	Antonio Moreno
4	AROUT	Around the Horn	Thomas Hardy
5	BERGS	Berglunds snabbköp	Christina Berglund

You'll need to use a different wildcard to search for specific digits within the code. The _ (underscore) wildcard matches any single character.

5 **Modify the query to search for customers with R and C as the second and fourth digits of their ID code.**

Modify the query to:

```
SELECT *
FROM Northwind.dbo.Customers
WHERE CustomerID LIKE '_R_C_'
```

This will search for values with R as the second digit and C as the fourth. When you execute the query, the matching customer appears.

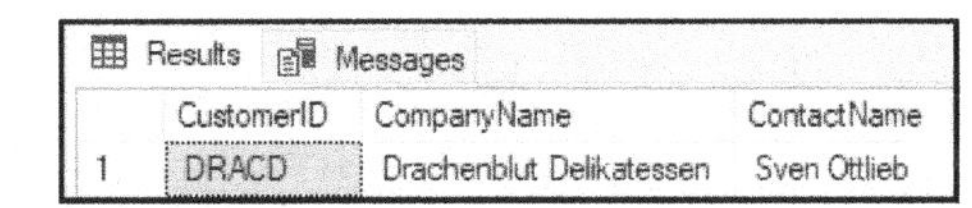

Results | Messages

	CustomerID	CompanyName	ContactName
1	DRACD	Drachenblut Delikatessen	Sven Ottlieb

You can use both % and _ within the same LIKE check.

Whether a LIKE check is case sensitive depends on how the database has been configured. SQL Server databases are not case sensitive by default.

note

Searching for ranges of letters or numbers

You can search for characters in a certain range of letters or numbers by enclosing them in square brackets.

For example, you can search for the letters a, b or c with:

```
LIKE '[abc]'
```

You can also use hyphens to search for ranges. The following code will also search for the letters a, b or c:

```
LIKE '[a-c]'
```

Finally, you can use the ! symbol to search for letters or numbers that are not in a certain range. For example, you can search for letters that are not a, b or c with:

```
LIKE '[!abc]'
```

Lesson 11: Use simple mathematical operators and custom column names

> **note**
>
> **Mathematical operators in SQL**
>
> SQL supports several mathematical operators, including:
>
> | | |
> |---|---|
> | **Add** | + |
> | **Subtract** | - |
> | **Divide** | / |
> | **Multiply** | * |
> | **Modulo** | % |
>
> The % operator is not used for percentages in SQL. Instead it performs a modulus calculation, which divides two numbers and returns the remainder after dividing. For example:
>
> **4%3=1**
>
> It's also important to note that the caret (^) operator is not used for exponential calculations and is instead used as the 'exclusive or' logical operator. You'll learn more about logical operators later in the course.
>
> SQL also contains many built in mathematical 'functions' to enable more advanced calculations, including exponents. You'll also learn about these later in the course, in: *Lesson 18: Use date functions.*

The SQL language supports all of the basic mathematical operators (see sidebar), allowing you to add, subtract, multiply and divide.

1 Open SSMS and connect to your SQL Server (if you haven't already done this).

2 Write a query to extract all records from the *Order Details* table.

You did this previously, in Lesson 8: Use the TOP and DISTINCT keywords.

The query should be:

```
SELECT *
FROM Northwind.dbo.[Order Details]
```

3 Execute the query.

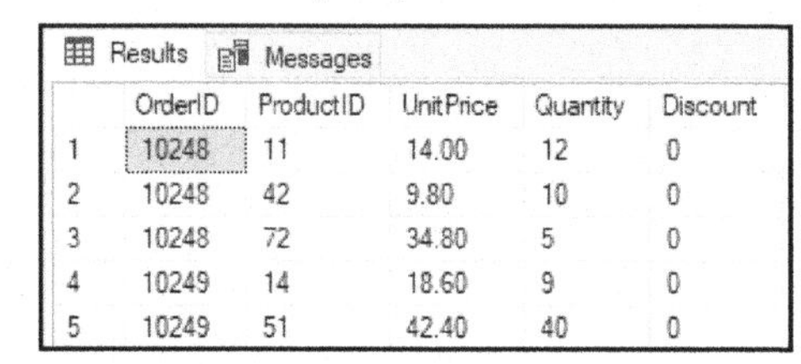

Results | Messages

	OrderID	ProductID	UnitPrice	Quantity	Discount
1	10248	11	14.00	12	0
2	10248	42	9.80	10	0
3	10248	72	34.80	5	0
4	10249	14	18.60	9	0
5	10249	51	42.40	40	0

Notice that the table contains the *UnitPrice* and the *Quantity*. To calculate the actual value of the order you will need to multiply the quantity and unit price.

4 Modify the query to calculate the order value.

The modified query should be:

```
SELECT *, UnitPrice*Quantity
FROM Northwind.dbo.[Order Details]
```

Notice that you can still add more items to the SELECT statement even when using * to return all columns from a table.

When used in mathematics, the * is the multiplication operator. SQL also supports several other operators (see sidebar).

5 Execute the query.

Results | Messages

	OrderID	ProductID	UnitPrice	Quantity	Discount	(No column name)
1	10248	11	14.00	12	0	168.00
2	10248	42	9.80	10	0	98.00
3	10248	72	34.80	5	0	174.00
4	10249	14	18.60	9	0	167.40
5	10249	51	42.40	40	0	1696.00

You can now see the order values in the last column but notice that the column is named *(No column name)*. You'll have to specify a custom column name to resolve this.

6 Use the AS keyword to set the column name to *OrderValue*.

You can use the AS keyword to specify a custom column name that will appear in your query results. This is often useful when you want to clarify your query results for other users or when you need to import your results into a different system.

Modify the query to:

```
SELECT *, UnitPrice*Quantity AS OrderValue
FROM Northwind.dbo.[Order Details]
```

> **note**
>
> **Custom column names with spaces**
>
> Just like with database tables and columns, you need to use square brackets to define a custom column name that has spaces.
>
> To set the column name to *Order Value* (rather than *OrderValue*) you would need to use the syntax:
>
> `UnitPrice*Quantity AS [Order Value]`

7 Execute the query.

Your custom column name appears in the query results, making it much clearer that the column contains the order value.

Results | Messages

	OrderID	ProductID	UnitPrice	Quantity	Discount	OrderValue
1	10248	11	14.00	12	0	168.00
2	10248	42	9.80	10	0	98.00
3	10248	72	34.80	5	0	174.00
4	10249	14	18.60	9	0	167.40
5	10249	51	42.40	40	0	1696.00

8 Modify the query to add an additional 10% to the OrderValue.

SQL supports the use of brackets to clarify the precedence of mathematical operations. Modify the formula to:

```
SELECT *, (UnitPrice*Quantity)*1.1 AS OrderValue
FROM Northwind.dbo.[Order Details]
```

Calculations in brackets are always done first. This means that the query will first multiply the *UnitPrice* and *Quantity* and then multiply the result of that calculation by 1.1 to get 110% of the value.

SQL Server calculates from left to right by default so the brackets aren't actually required in this case, but it is best practice to use brackets wherever the precedence could be ambiguous, especially if your code might be used on a different database server that could have different rules of precedence.

9 Execute the query.

10% is added to all of the values in the *OrderValue* column.

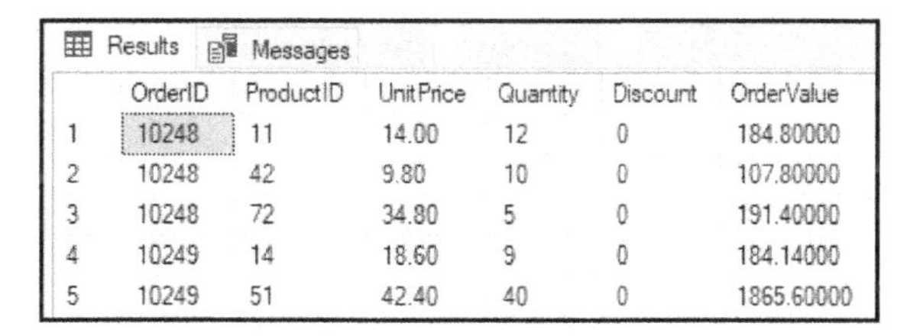

Results | Messages

	OrderID	ProductID	UnitPrice	Quantity	Discount	OrderValue
1	10248	11	14.00	12	0	184.80000
2	10248	42	9.80	10	0	107.80000
3	10248	72	34.80	5	0	191.40000
4	10249	14	18.60	9	0	184.14000
5	10249	51	42.40	40	0	1865.60000

Lesson 12: Concatenate text and numbers

In the previous lesson you used the + operator to add numbers together, but you can also use it to concatenate text. Joining pieces of text together can be useful for many different purposes (see sidebar). You'll also see how to split text later in the course, in: *Lesson 19: Work with text functions.*

note

Practical applications

The most obvious practical application of concatenating text is for display purposes, but it can also be very useful for a programmer.

You can use text concatenation to generate code and scripts from your database. For example, you could create rows in an HTML table using the code:

```
SELECT '<tr><td>' +
FirstName +
'</tr></td>'
```

1. Open SSMS and connect to your SQL Server (if you haven't already done this).

2. Write a query to extract the *TitleOfCourtesy*, *FirstName* and *LastName* from the *Employees* table.

   The query should be:

```
SELECT TitleOfCourtesy, FirstName, LastName
FROM Northwind.dbo.Employees
```

3. Execute the query.

   The titles, first names and last names are displayed.

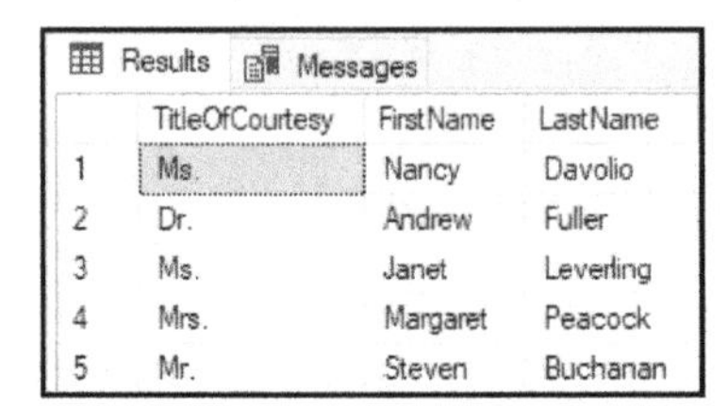

Results | Messages

	TitleOfCourtesy	FirstName	LastName
1	Ms.	Nancy	Davolio
2	Dr.	Andrew	Fuller
3	Ms.	Janet	Leverling
4	Mrs.	Margaret	Peacock
5	Mr.	Steven	Buchanan

   Your goal is to join the three columns together to create a single column containing the complete name.

4. Write a query to concatenate the title, first name and last name into a single column.

   You can use the + operator to join pieces of text together. As you saw in *Lesson 9: Filter results with WHERE,* text needs to be enclosed in single quote marks.

   The query should look like this:

```
SELECT
TitleOfCourtesy + ' ' + FirstName + ' ' + LastName AS
FullName
FROM Northwind.dbo.Employees
```

5. Execute the query.

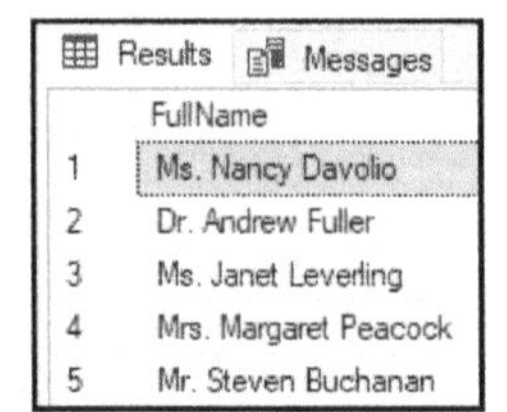

Results | Messages

	FullName
1	Ms. Nancy Davolio
2	Dr. Andrew Fuller
3	Ms. Janet Leverling
4	Mrs. Margaret Peacock
5	Mr. Steven Buchanan

6. Execute a query to concatenate the word *Employee* and the *EmployeeID*.

Each database column has a specific data type. The *EmployeeID* column is an *int* (integer) column, which means it can only contain whole numbers and cannot contain text.

1. Try executing the following query:

```
SELECT 'Employee: ' + EmployeeID AS Employee
FROM Northwind.dbo.Employees
```

   An error message is displayed.

```
Results   Messages
Msg 245, Level 16, State 1, Line 1
Conversion failed when converting the varchar value 'Employee: ' to data type int.
```

   This message tells you (in a rather cryptic way) that you are trying to concatenate two incompatible data types. A piece of text in single quotes is considered to be the *varchar* data type (the most common text type), while the *EmployeeID* has the *int* data type.

   To concatenate the two values you will need to convert the *EmployeeID* into a textual type. You can do this with the *CAST* function.

2. Modify the query to:

```
SELECT
'Employee: ' + CAST(EmployeeID as varchar) AS
Employee
FROM Northwind.dbo.Employees
```

   You can use CAST to attempt to convert to any data type (see sidebar for a full list of data types). CAST will fail if you try to perform an impossible conversion, such as converting a piece of text into a number.

   You can also convert between types using the CONVERT function. You'll use CONVERT later in the course.

3. Execute the query.

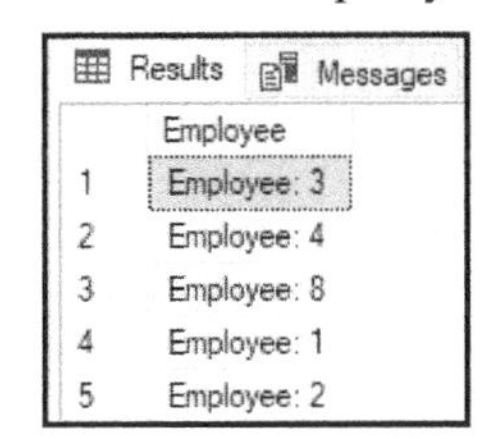

Results | Messages

	Employee
1	Employee: 3
2	Employee: 4
3	Employee: 8
4	Employee: 1
5	Employee: 2

   You have successfully concatenated the two items.

note

The data types available in SQL Server

SQL Server contains the following data types:

int, bigint, smallint, tinyint
Used for whole numbers.

bit
Only contains 1 or 0 (often shown as *True* and *False*).

char, nchar, nvarchar, varchar, text, ntext
Used for textual values.

date, datetime, datetime2, datetimeoffset, smalldatetime, time, timestamp
Used for dates and times.

decimal, numeric, float, money, smallmoney, real
Used for decimal numbers.

binary, varbinary and image
Used to store files and images.

uniqueidentifier
A special data type for unique identifier codes.

xml
Used to store XML code.

sql_variant
A special data type that can store multiple types of data. Any data stored in a *sql_variant* column will need to be converted into a different type using CAST or CONVERT before it can be used.

Note that different database engines have different sets of data types. For example, MySQL uses a data type called *BLOB* as an alternative to the *binary* type used by SQL Server.

Lesson 13: Understand dates and use the CONVERT function

Databases usually store dates as a number of days from a particular date. The start date varies according to the data type, but it is the *1st of January 1900* for most types.

This means dates can be easily added to and subtracted from, and that dates can be easily added together. SQL Server also offers the *DATEADD* function which you'll use later, in: *Lesson 18: Use date functions*.

note

Date style options

The following date style options are available in SQL Server.

100	mon dd yyyy hh:miAM/PM
101	mm/dd/yyyy
102	yyyy.mm.dd
103	dd/mm/yyyy
104	dd.mm.yyyy
105	dd-mm-yyyy
106	dd mon yyyy
107	Mon dd, yyyy
108	hh:mm:ss
109	mon dd yyyy hh:mi:ss:mmmAM
110	mm-dd-yyyy
111	yyyy/mm/dd
112	yyyymmdd
113	dd mon yyyy hh:mi:ss:mmm
114	hh:mi:ss:mmm
120	yyyy-mm-dd hh:mi:ss
121	yyyy-mm-dd hh:mi:ss.mmm
126	yyyy-mm-dd Thh:mi:ss.mmm
127	yyyy-mm-dd Thh:mi:ss.mmmZ
130	dd mon yyyy hh:mi:ss:mmmAM
131	dd/mm/yy hh:mi:ss:mmmAM

Subtracting 100 from the style code will display 2 digits for the year rather than 4. For example, *101* returns *mm/dd/yyyy*, while *1* returns *mm/dd/yy*.

Different database engines (such as MySQL) have different versions of the CONVERT function that may not allow styles to be applied in the same way.

1. Open SSMS and connect to your SQL Server (if you haven't already done this).

2. Execute a query to display all the *OrderID* and *OrderDate* values from the *Orders* table.

   Run the following query:

```
SELECT OrderID, OrderDate
FROM Northwind.dbo.Orders
```

	OrderID	OrderDate
1	10248	1996-07-04 00:00:00.000
2	10249	1996-07-05 00:00:00.000
3	10250	1996-07-08 00:00:00.000
4	10251	1996-07-08 00:00:00.000
5	10252	1996-07-09 00:00:00.000

   You can see at a glance that the *OrderDate* column contains dates and times.

3. Modify the query to display a *DueDate* column containing a date 30 days later than the *OrderDate*.

   Because dates are actually simple numbers, you can easily add days to them. Run the following query:

```
SELECT
OrderID, OrderDate, OrderDate+30 AS DueDate
FROM Northwind.dbo.Orders
```

   The *DueDate* column works correctly.

Results | Messages

	OrderID	OrderDate	DueDate
1	10248	1996-07-04 00:00:00.000	1996-08-03 00:00:00.000
2	10249	1996-07-05 00:00:00.000	1996-08-04 00:00:00.000
3	10250	1996-07-08 00:00:00.000	1996-08-07 00:00:00.000
4	10251	1996-07-08 00:00:00.000	1996-08-07 00:00:00.000
5	10252	1996-07-09 00:00:00.000	1996-08-08 00:00:00.000

4. Use the CONVERT function to display the date in the US standard format.

   The CONVERT function is very similar to the CAST function. The difference is that CONVERT allows you to specify a style when converting dates into text.

   Run the following query:

```
SELECT
OrderID,
CONVERT(varchar, OrderDate, 101) AS USOrderDate
FROM Northwind.dbo.Orders
```

As you can see, you're using the *CONVERT* function to convert the *OrderDate* to the *varchar* date type (the most common text type).

The *101* part of the function specifies that you want the date to be displayed in the US standard format (Month/Day/Year), including the century. There are many other style options available (see sidebar).

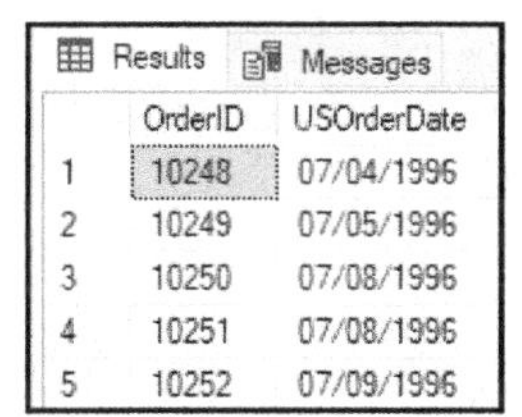

	OrderID	USOrderDate
1	10248	07/04/1996
2	10249	07/05/1996
3	10250	07/08/1996
4	10251	07/08/1996
5	10252	07/09/1996

You can also use the CONVERT function in place of the CAST function. For example, *CAST(OrderID as varchar)* and *CONVERT(varchar, OrderID)* have exactly the same effect.

5 Modify the query to concatenate the *OrderID* with the formatted order date, using the CONVERT function.

The query should be:

```
SELECT
CONVERT(varchar, OrderID) + ' - ' + CONVERT(varchar,
OrderDate, 101) AS USOrderDate
FROM Northwind.dbo.Orders
```

You saw how to do the same thing in: *Lesson 12: Concatenate text and numbers.*

6 Execute the query.

The text is concatenated successfully.

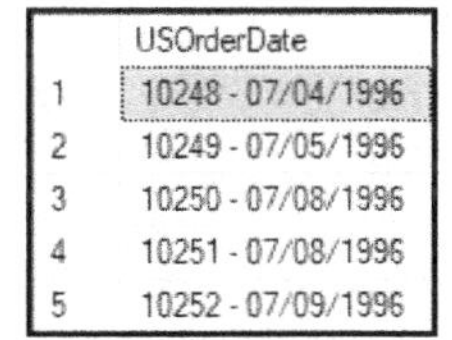

	USOrderDate
1	10248 - 07/04/1996
2	10249 - 07/05/1996
3	10250 - 07/08/1996
4	10251 - 07/08/1996
5	10252 - 07/09/1996

Lesson 14: Use logical operators and filter by date

You've already used the WHERE statement to apply a single criteria in: *Lesson 9: Filter results with WHERE.* In this lesson you will use logical operators to apply multiple criteria and more complex logic. One of the most common uses for this is to filter results by a range of dates.

1 Open SSMS and connect to your SQL Server (if you haven't already done this).

2 Execute a query to display all records from the *Orders* table for EmployeeID 5.

```
SELECT *
FROM Northwind.dbo.Orders
WHERE EmployeeID=5
```

You saw how to do this in: *Lesson 9: Filter results with WHERE.*

	OrderID	CustomerID	EmployeeID	OrderDate
1	10248	VINET	5	1996-07-04 00:00:00.000
2	10254	CHOPS	5	1996-07-11 00:00:00.000
3	10269	WHITC	5	1996-07-31 00:00:00.000
4	10297	BLONP	5	1996-09-04 00:00:00.000
5	10320	WARTH	5	1996-10-03 00:00:00.000

If you examine the results you can see that there are 42 records spanning 3 years.

3 Modify the query to only display orders from 1997.

You can use the AND logical operator to apply multiple filters. Modify the query to:

```
SELECT *
FROM Northwind.dbo.Orders
WHERE EmployeeID=5
AND OrderDate >= '01 Jan 1997'
AND OrderDate < '01 Jan 1998'
```

You WHERE statement is now telling the server that you only want records where the *EmployeeID* is 5 and the *OrderDate* is on or later than the 1st of January 1997 and the *OrderDate* is earlier than the 1st of January 1998.

4 Execute the query.

The results are filtered correctly.

	OrderID	CustomerID	EmployeeID	OrderDate
1	10463	SUPRD	5	1997-03-04 00:00:00.000
2	10474	PERIC	5	1997-03-13 00:00:00.000
3	10477	PRINI	5	1997-03-17 00:00:00.000
4	10529	MAISD	5	1997-05-07 00:00:00.000
5	10549	QUICK	5	1997-05-27 00:00:00.000

note

Applying date ranges with BETWEEN

In this lesson you applied a date range filter using the AND logical operator, but you can also use the BETWEEN operator to do the same thing.

To apply the same date range used in the lesson you could use:

```
WHERE OrderDate BETWEEN
'01 Jan 1997' AND
'31 Dec 1997'
```

This also works with numerical values.

This kind of date filter always includes the start and finish date in the results, making it a little less flexible than the technique shown in the lesson.

5 Modify the query to also display records for EmployeeID 6.

The OR operator allows you to specify that a record should be displayed if one of several criteria are true.

1. Modify the query to:

```
SELECT *
FROM Northwind.dbo.Orders
WHERE EmployeeID=5
OR EmployeeID=6
AND OrderDate >= '01 Jan 1997'
AND OrderDate < '01 Jan 1998'
```

2. Execute the query.

Results | Messages

	OrderID	CustomerID	EmployeeID	OrderDate
1	10248	VINET	5	1996-07-04 00:00:00.000
2	10254	CHOPS	5	1996-07-11 00:00:00.000
3	10269	WHITC	5	1996-07-31 00:00:00.000
4	10297	BLONP	5	1996-09-04 00:00:00.000
5	10320	WARTH	5	1996-10-03 00:00:00.000

The results aren't quite what you wanted. Records from 1996 are now being displayed. This is because it's not clear which order the rules should be processed in. The server thinks you want to see all records for EmployeeID 5, regardless of which year they are in. Just like with mathematical expressions, you need to use brackets to clarify precedence.

3. Modify the query to:

```
SELECT *
FROM Northwind.dbo.Orders
WHERE
(EmployeeID=5 OR EmployeeID=6)
AND
(OrderDate >= '01 Jan 1997'
AND OrderDate < '01 Jan 1998')
```

The brackets clarify that you want the database to return records where the *EmployeeID* is 5 or 6 and where the date is on or later than the 1st of January 1997 and the date is less than the 1st of January 1998.

4. Execute the query.

Results | Messages

	OrderID	CustomerID	EmployeeID	OrderDate
4	10446	TOMSP	6	1997-02-14 00:00:00.000
5	10463	SUPRD	5	1997-03-04 00:00:00.000
6	10474	PERIC	5	1997-03-13 00:00:00.000
7	10477	PRINI	5	1997-03-17 00:00:00.000
8	10480	FOLIG	6	1997-03-20 00:00:00.000

The results are now correct.

note

<> and the NOT operator

When you want to check if a number is not equal to a value, you can use <>. For example, to find values where the *EmployeeID* is not 5 you could use:

```
WHERE EmployeeID<>5
```

The NOT operator is used to create logical tests for things that are not true. For example, you can extract orders that were not in 1997 with:

```
WHERE NOT (
OrderDate >= '01 Jan 1997'
AND OrderDate < '01 Jan 1998')
```

Lesson 15: Use aggregate functions and GROUP BY

It's common to need to produce reports with grouped subtotals such as total sales by customer or average sales by country. SQL offers several functions to enable this, known as *aggregate* functions.

Aggregate functions combine values from multiple records into a single value.

1. Open SSMS and connect to your SQL Server (if you haven't already done this).

2. Execute a query to show the total number of units in stock from the *Products* table.

   The SUM function allows you to extract a total value from multiple records.

   Execute the following query:

```
SELECT SUM(UnitsInStock) AS TotalUnitsInStock
FROM Northwind.dbo.Products
```

   The results show that there are 3119 units in stock across all products and suppliers.

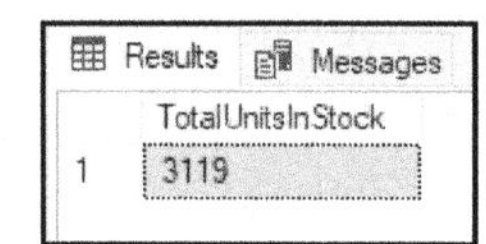

   The SUM function has added together the *UnitsInStock* values from every record.

   The results of aggregate functions don't have a column title by default, so you've used a custom column name. You learned about these in: *Lesson 11: Use simple mathematical operators and custom column names.*

3. Modify the query to display the total units in stock by *SupplierID*.

   When you want to group aggregated values together you need to use the *GROUP BY* statement. GROUP BY comes after the SELECT, FROM and WHERE statements, but before the ORDER BY statement.

   1. Modify the query to:

```
SELECT SupplierID,
SUM(UnitsInStock) AS TotalUnitsInStock
FROM Northwind.dbo.Products
```

   2. Execute the query.

      An error message is displayed.

```
Messages
Msg 8120, Level 16, State 1, Line 1
Column 'Products.SupplierID' is invalid in the select list
because it is not contained in either an aggregate function
or the GROUP BY clause.
```

note

Other aggregate functions

The following aggregate functions are available in most database engines (not just SQL Server):

AVG
Returns the average of all values.

SUM
Adds all values together.

COUNT
Counts the number of items.

MAX
Returns the highest value.

MIN
Returns the lowest value.

SQL Server also offers some more advanced aggregate functions that aren't available in many other databases.

COUNT_BIG
Returns a count using the *bigint* data type.

STDEV and **STDEVP**
Returns the standard deviation. STDEVP should be used when calculating the standard deviation of all records in a table, while STDEV should be used when working with a sample of records.

VAR and **VARP**
Returns the statistical variance. VARP should be used when calculating the variance of all records in a table, while VAR should be used when working with a sample of records.

This error message is telling you that *SupplierID* needs to be included in the *GROUP BY* statement for this query to be valid.

If you use both ordinary columns (columns that aren't being aggregated) and aggregate functions in the SELECT statement you must include all ordinary columns in the GROUP BY statement to specify that they should be treated as grouping levels.

The reason this is necessary is because it is possible to enter columns in the GROUP BY statement that are not in the SELECT statement.

3. Modify the query to:

```
SELECT SupplierID,
SUM(UnitsInStock) AS TotalUnitsInStock
FROM Northwind.dbo.Products
GROUP BY SupplierID
```

4. Execute the query.

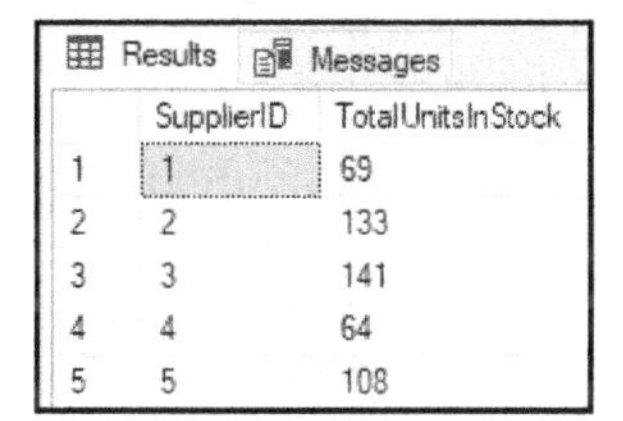

Results | Messages

	SupplierID	TotalUnitsInStock
1	1	69
2	2	133
3	3	141
4	4	64
5	5	108

The total units in stock by supplier are displayed.

4 Modify the query to display the total units in stock by *SupplierID* and *CategoryID*.

1. Modify the query to:

```
SELECT SupplierID, CategoryID,
SUM(UnitsInStock) AS TotalUnitsInStock
FROM Northwind.dbo.Products
GROUP BY SupplierID, CategoryID
ORDER BY SupplierID, CategoryID
```

2. Execute the query.

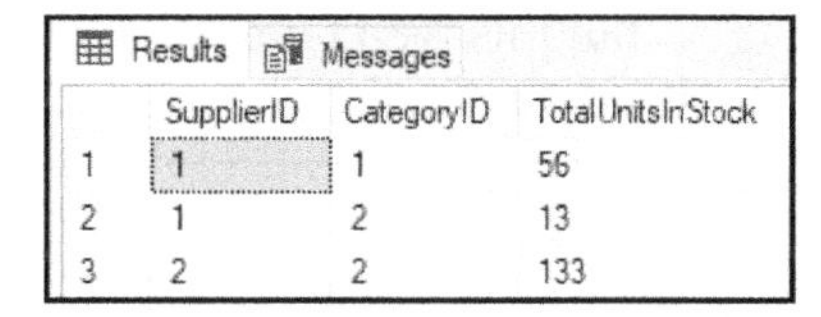

Results | Messages

	SupplierID	CategoryID	TotalUnitsInStock
1	1	1	56
2	1	2	13
3	2	2	133

The total units in stock are now shown by supplier and category. Notice that *ORDER BY* is placed after *GROUP BY*.

SQL Server also offers several other aggregate functions (see sidebar).

note

NULL values can be disallowed

The database's designer can specify whether table columns are 'nullable' or not. Some database designers prefer to avoid null values and instead replace them with values such as 'Unknown'.

Even if null values aren't allowed in tables you can still encounter null values when joining tables together. You'll see this happening in: *Lesson 23: Use full joins.*

Lesson 16: Work with NULL values and the IN keyword

Databases have a concept of 'null'. NULL indicates that an item does not have a value. A NULL value is not the same as a value of zero. NULL values are ignored by aggregate functions like SUM and AVG and need to be specifically filtered for.

The IN keyword allows you to easily filter for multiple conditions without needing multiple AND statements.

In this lesson you'll see how to filter out NULL values and use the IN keyword to simplify your WHERE criteria.

1. Open SSMS and connect to your SQL Server (if you haven't already done this).

2. Execute a query to extract the *CompanyName, Country* and *PostalCode* from the *Customers* table.

   Execute the following query:

```
SELECT CompanyName, Country, PostalCode
FROM Northwind.dbo.Customers
ORDER BY CompanyName
```

   Notice that the postal code for *Hungry Owl All-Night Grocers* is *NULL*.

	CompanyName	Country	PostalCode
38	Hungry Owl All-Night Grocers	Ireland	NULL
39	Island Trading	UK	PO31 7PJ
40	Königlich Essen	Germany	14776

3. Modify the query to exclude values with *NULL* postal codes.

   Filtering out null values requires a slightly unusual syntax. You might think you could use the code:

```
WHERE PostalCode <> NULL
```

   ...but this won't work. To exclude null values, you will need to modify the query to:

```
SELECT CompanyName, Country, PostalCode
FROM Northwind.dbo.Customers
WHERE PostalCode IS NOT NULL
ORDER BY CompanyName
```

   Hungry Owl All-Night Grocers is now excluded from the results.

	CompanyName	Country	PostalCode
38	Island Trading	UK	PO31 7PJ
39	Königlich Essen	Germany	14776
40	La come d'abondance	France	78000

4. Modify the query to only show customers in the *USA, Canada, Mexico, Brazil* and *Argentina*.

You could do this using 5 different OR statements, with the following query:

```
SELECT CompanyName, Country, PostalCode
FROM Northwind.dbo.Customers
WHERE PostalCode IS NOT NULL
AND (Country ='USA' OR Country='Canada'
OR Country='Mexico' OR Country='Brazil'
OR Country='Argentina')
ORDER BY CompanyName
```

This will work, but the IN keyword allows you to do the same thing with less code.

Modify the query to:

```
SELECT CompanyName, Country, PostalCode
FROM Northwind.dbo.Customers
WHERE PostalCode IS NOT NULL
AND Country IN
('USA','Canada','Mexico','Brazil','Argentina')
ORDER BY CompanyName
```

The results of the query show all customers in the specified countries.

	CompanyName	Country	PostalCode
1	Ana Trujillo Emparedados y helados	Mexico	05021
2	Antonio Moreno Taquería	Mexico	05023
3	Bottom-Dollar Markets	Canada	T2F 8M4

5 Modify the query to only show customers not in the *USA, Canada, Mexico, Brazil* and *Argentina*.

The *IN* keyword also works with the *NOT* operator. You can very easily extract the customers not in the Americas with the query:

```
SELECT CompanyName, Country, PostalCode
FROM Northwind.dbo.Customers
WHERE PostalCode IS NOT NULL
AND Country NOT IN
('USA','Canada','Mexico','Brazil','Argentina')
ORDER BY CompanyName
```

The results show customers in all other countries.

	CompanyName	Country	PostalCode
1	Alfreds Futterkiste	Germany	12209
2	Around the Horn	UK	WA1 1DP
3	Berglunds snabbköp	Sweden	S-958 22

The *IN* keyword is very useful for easily filtering for multiple conditions. It can also be extremely useful when used alongside subqueries, which you'll learn about in: *Lesson 26: Work with subqueries*.

Lesson 17: Use the HAVING statement to filter aggregate results

HAVING is the only major SQL statement you haven't encountered at this point. It's used to create filters based on the results of aggregate functions.

Filters in the WHERE statement are applied to each individual record before any aggregates are calculated. If you want to create a filter that's applied after the calculation you need to use HAVING.

1 Open SSMS and connect to your SQL Server (if you haven't already done this).

2 Execute a query to display the average *Quantity* sold by *ProductID* from the *Order Details* table by product.

You saw how to create a grouped subtotal in: *Lesson 15: Use aggregate functions and GROUP BY.* The query should be:

```
SELECT
ProductID, AVG(Quantity) AS AverageQuantity
FROM Northwind.dbo.[Order Details]
GROUP BY ProductID
ORDER BY AverageQuantity DESC
```

Notice that you can use custom column names in the *ORDER BY* statement. 77 results are shown, with the products that have the highest average quantity sold per order displayed first.

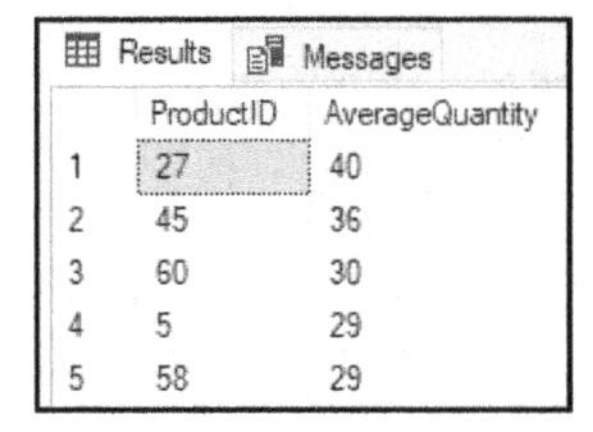

	ProductID	AverageQuantity
1	27	40
2	45	36
3	60	30
4	5	29
5	58	29

3 Modify the query to only show products with an average quantity per order higher than 28.

1. Modify the query to:

```
SELECT ProductID,
AVG(Quantity) AS AverageQuantity
FROM Northwind.dbo.[Order Details]
WHERE Quantity > 28
GROUP BY ProductID
ORDER BY AverageQuantity DESC
```

Notice that the WHERE statement needs to be placed between the FROM and GROUP BY statements.

2. Execute the query.

note

You can use logical operators in the HAVING statement

You can use logical operators in the HAVING statement just like you used in the WHERE statement in: *Lesson 14: Use logical operators and filter by date.*

Results | Messages

	ProductID	AverageQuantity
1	48	70
2	53	64
3	44	61
4	61	61
5	37	60

This isn't the result you wanted. 77 records are still returned, but the averages have now been calculated based only on sales with quantities greater than 28. To filter the values in the *AverageQuantity* column you will need to use the *HAVING* statement.

3. Modify the query to:

```
SELECT ProductID,
AVG(Quantity) AS AverageQuantity
FROM Northwind.dbo.[Order Details]
GROUP BY ProductID
HAVING AVG(Quantity) > 28
ORDER BY AverageQuantity DESC
```

The *HAVING* statement is always placed after the *GROUP BY* statement, but before *ORDER BY*.

4. Execute the query.

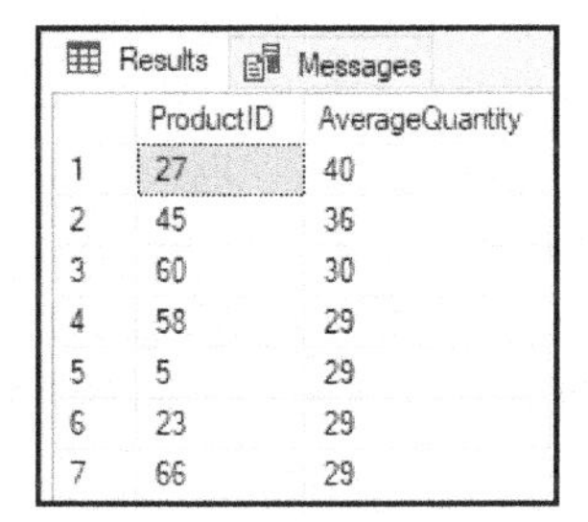

Results | Messages

	ProductID	AverageQuantity
1	27	40
2	45	36
3	60	30
4	58	29
5	5	29
6	23	29
7	66	29

The 7 records you wanted are now displayed.

4 Modify the query to exclude orders with discounts.

1. Modify the query to:

```
SELECT ProductID,
AVG(Quantity) AS AverageQuantity
FROM Northwind.dbo.[Order Details]
WHERE Discount=0
GROUP BY ProductID
HAVING AVG(Quantity) > 28
ORDER BY AverageQuantity DESC
```

2. Execute the query.

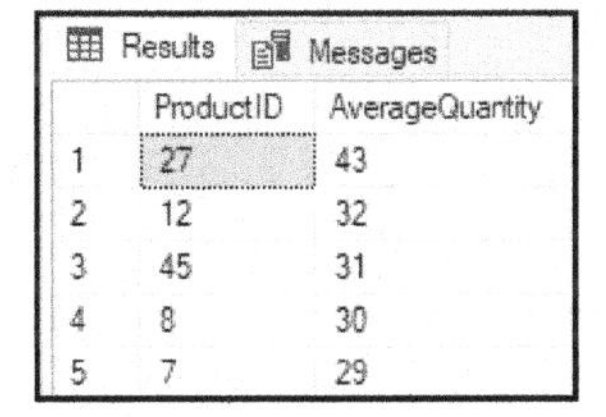

Results | Messages

	ProductID	AverageQuantity
1	27	43
2	12	32
3	45	31
4	8	30
5	7	29

The results are displayed.

Lesson 18: Use date functions

You've already worked with several of SQL Server's functions. Unlike the aggregate functions you worked with in *Lesson 15: Use aggregate functions and GROUP BY*, most functions apply to every row in the table.

There are 82 functions available in SQL Server, but different database engines such as MySQL have different sets of functions.

This course won't cover every available function, but you will work with the most useful functions that are most likely to be available in different databases.

1. Open SSMS and connect to your SQL Server (if you haven't already done this).

2. Execute a query to extract the *OrderID* and *OrderDate* from the *Orders* table.

   The query should be:

```
SELECT OrderID, OrderDate
FROM Northwind.dbo.Orders
```

Results | Messages

	OrderID	OrderDate
1	10248	1996-07-04 00:00:00.000
2	10249	1996-07-05 00:00:00.000
3	10250	1996-07-08 00:00:00.000
4	10251	1996-07-08 00:00:00.000
5	10252	1996-07-09 00:00:00.000

3. Use the DATEADD function to calculate a *CollectionsDate* that is 1 year later than the *OrderDate*.

   You've added days to dates previously, in *Lesson 13: Understand dates and use the CONVERT function*. The DATEADD function enables you to add days, months and years to a date, as well as several other intervals (see sidebar).

   The query you need is:

```
SELECT OrderID,
DATEADD(year, 1, OrderDate) AS CollectionsDate
FROM Northwind.dbo.Orders
```

This DATEADD function adds *1 year* to the *OrderDate*.

DATEADD is implemented differently in different databases such as MySQL.

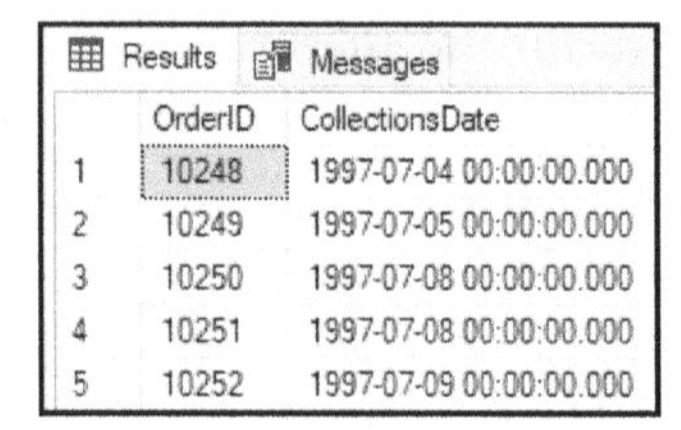

Results | Messages

	OrderID	CollectionsDate
1	10248	1997-07-04 00:00:00.000
2	10249	1997-07-05 00:00:00.000
3	10250	1997-07-08 00:00:00.000
4	10251	1997-07-08 00:00:00.000
5	10252	1997-07-09 00:00:00.000

The dates are all incremented by 1 year.

note

Mathematical functions

SQL Server offers a large library of mathematical functions. These work in the same way as the date functions shown in this lesson and the text functions shown in the next lesson.

ABS()
Returns the absolute value of a number (converts negative numbers to positive).

CEIL() and **FLOOR()**
Applies a floor or ceiling to a value.

MOD()
Applies a modulus to the number. You can also do this with the % operator as shown in: *Lesson 11: Use simple mathematical operators and custom column names.*

ROUND()
Rounds a number to a specified number of decimal places.

EXP(), **POW()** and **POWER()**
Apply exponents to a number.

RAND()
Returns a random value between 0 and 1.

SQRT
Gets the square root of a value.

There are also several other functions available. You can find a full list in Microsoft's documentation.

note

DATEADD options

The following options work with the DATEADD function:

day, dy, y	Days.
week, ww, wk	Weeks.
month, mm, m	Months.
quarter, qq, q	Quarters.
year, yyyy, yy	Years.
hour, hh	Hours.
minute, mi, n	Minutes.
second, ss, s	Seconds.
millisecond, ms	Milliseconds.

4 Use the YEAR, MONTH and DAY functions to split the *OrderDate* into three columns.

The YEAR, MONTH and DAY functions allow you to extract specific parts of a date. Modify the query to:

```
SELECT OrderID,
YEAR(OrderDate) AS Year,
MONTH(OrderDate) AS Month,
DAY(OrderDate) AS Day
FROM Northwind.dbo.Orders
```

The results show the year month and day in separate columns.

Results | Messages

	OrderID	Year	Month	Day
1	10248	1996	7	4
2	10249	1996	7	5
3	10250	1996	7	8
4	10251	1996	7	8
5	10252	1996	7	9

You'll notice that the words *Year, Month* and *Day* are highlighted in pink. This is because they are recognized as the names of SQL functions.

You can clarify that they are custom column names and prevent the highlighting by enclosing them in square brackets, as you saw in: *Lesson 6: Understand the SELECT statement and save a query*.

5 Use the YEAR function in the WHERE statement to display records from 1997.

You can use date functions in the WHERE statement, which gives you an additional option for date filtering (although it is less efficient).

Modify the query to:

```
SELECT OrderID,
YEAR(OrderDate) AS Year,
MONTH(OrderDate) AS Month,
DAY(OrderDate) AS Day
FROM Northwind.dbo.Orders
WHERE YEAR(OrderDate)=1997
```

Only records from 1997 are shown.

Results | Messages

	OrderID	Year	Month	Day
1	10400	1997	1	1
2	10401	1997	1	1
3	10402	1997	1	2
4	10403	1997	1	3
5	10404	1997	1	3

Although there is more than one way to filter by date, the techniques that you learned earlier result in faster and more efficient queries than others. You'll see how to analyze and optimize your queries in: *Lesson 30: Analyze and optimize a query*.

Lesson 19: Work with text functions

You worked with SQL's date functions in *Lesson 18: Use date functions*. SQL also includes many functions that work with textual values.

1 Open SSMS and connect to your SQL Server (if you haven't already done this).

2 Execute a query to extract the *HomePhone* number from the *Employees* table.

The query you need is:

```
SELECT HomePhone
FROM Northwind.dbo.Employees
```

Notice that the phone numbers contain brackets and hyphens.

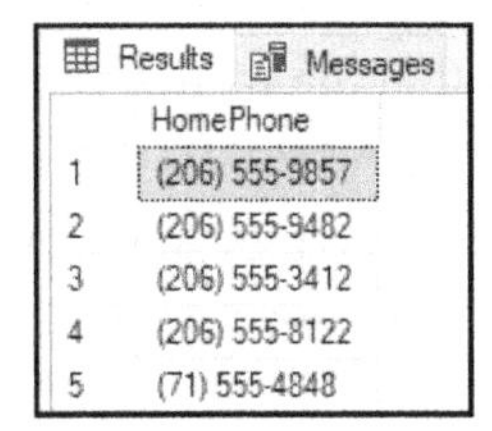
Results | Messages

	HomePhone
1	(206) 555-9857
2	(206) 555-9482
3	(206) 555-3412
4	(206) 555-8122
5	(71) 555-4848

3 Use the *REPLACE* function to remove the hyphens from the phone numbers.

The REPLACE function allows you to 'find and replace' text within database columns.

Modify the query to:

```
SELECT REPLACE(HomePhone, '-', '')
FROM Northwind.dbo.Employees
```

As usual, you need to use single quote marks for textual values. You are telling the REPLACE function to find all hyphens (-) and replace them with nothing (an empty set of single quotes).

When you execute the query, you can see that the hyphens are removed.

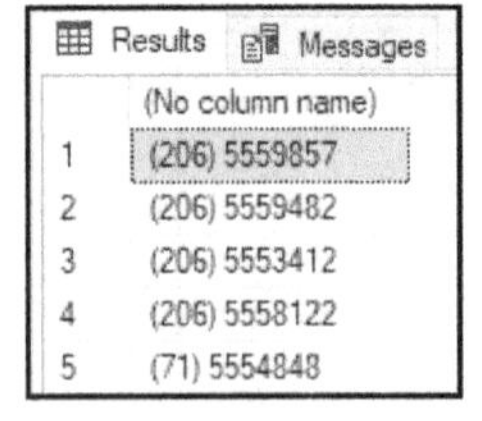
Results | Messages

	(No column name)
1	(206) 5559857
2	(206) 5559482
3	(206) 5553412
4	(206) 5558122
5	(71) 5554848

4 Use the *RIGHT* function to extract the last 4 digits of the phone numbers.

The *RIGHT* function extracts a certain number of characters from the end of a piece of text (the right side). The LEFT function is similar but extracting text from the beginning (the left side).

Modify the query to:

note

Other text functions

SQL Server contains many other text functions, but two of the most useful are the *LEN* and *SUBSTRING* functions.

LEN extracts the length of a string. For example, the result of *LEN*('sqlserver') would be 9.

SUBSTRING is similar to *LEFT* and *RIGHT*, but it enables you to extract text from any position within a string rather than just the start or end. To get the word *server* from *sqlserver*, you could use:

SUBSTRING('sqlserver',4,6)

The LEN, CHARINDEX and SUBSTRING functions are often combined to search for and extract specific parts of pieces of text.

SQL Server also contains several additional text functions that have more specialized purposes. You can find a complete list in Microsoft's documentation.

```
SELECT RIGHT(REPLACE(HomePhone, '-', ''),7)
FROM Northwind.dbo.Employees
```

The last 7 digits are extracted.

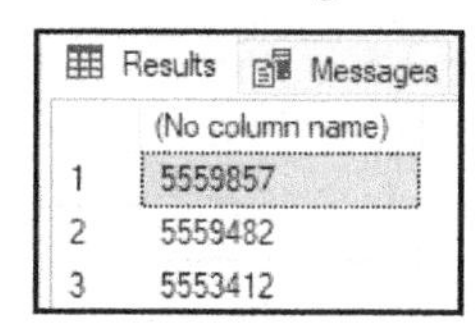

5 Use the *CHARINDEX* function to find the position of the ending bracket in the phone numbers.

CHARINDEX allows you to search a piece of text for a particular letter or group of letters and return its position in the text.

Modify the query to:

```
SELECT RIGHT(REPLACE(HomePhone, '-', ''),7),
HomePhone, CHARINDEX(')',HomePhone)
FROM Northwind.dbo.Employees
```

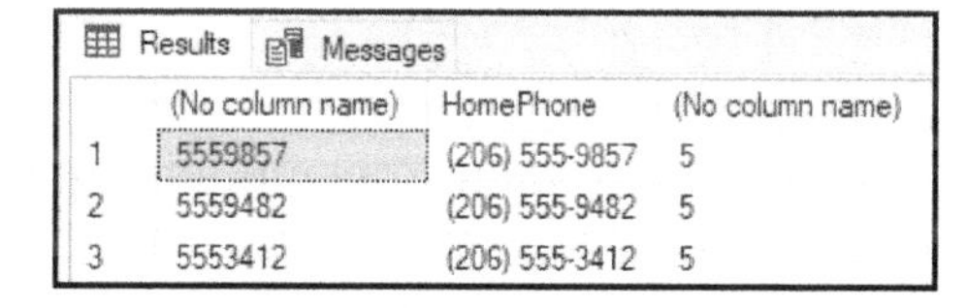

The numbers indicate the position of the ending bracket. You can see that it is the 5th character in some records and the 4th in others.

6 Use the *LEFT* function to extract the area codes.

Now that you know where the ending brackets are, you can use the LEFT function to extract the numbers in brackets.

Modify the query to:

```
SELECT LEFT(HomePhone, CHARINDEX(')',HomePhone)),
RIGHT(REPLACE(HomePhone, '-', ''),7)
FROM Northwind.dbo.Employees
```

The area codes and phone numbers are displayed in separate columns.

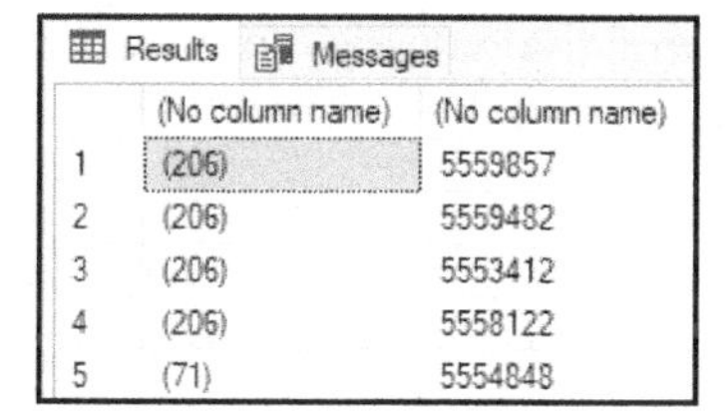

Lesson 20: Understand relationships

All of the queries you have written so far have worked with a single table. You'll need a deeper understanding of how databases work before you can go further and begin to extract data from multiple tables.

1 Open SSMS and connect to your SQL Server (if you haven't already done this).

2 Examine the contents of the *Orders* table.

You can do this either by writing a simple query or by right-clicking on the table in SSMS and clicking *Select Top 1000 Rows* from the shortcut menu, as you did in: *Lesson 4: Explore a database.*

Results | Messages

	OrderID	CustomerID	EmployeeID	OrderDate
1	10248	VINET	5	1996-07-04 00:00:00.000
2	10249	TOMSP	6	1996-07-05 00:00:00.000
3	10250	HANAR	4	1996-07-08 00:00:00.000
4	10251	VICTE	3	1996-07-08 00:00:00.000
5	10252	SUPRD	4	1996-07-09 00:00:00.000

The *Order* table contains information about sales orders. The *CustomerID* and *EmployeeID* columns contain ID numbers that indicate which customer the sale was to and which employee made the sale.

The *Orders* table doesn't contain in-depth information about customers and employees. That information is held in the *Customers* and *Employees* tables.

3 Examine the contents of the *Customers* table.

The *Customers* table contains information about each customer.

Results | Messages

	CustomerID	CompanyName	ContactName
84	VICTE	Victuailles en stock	Mary Saveley
85	VINET	Vins et alcools Chevalier	Paul Henriot
86	WANDK	Die Wandernde Kuh	Rita Müller
87	WARTH	Wartian Herkku	Pirkko Koskitalo

Notice that the *CustomerID* column corresponds to the *CustomerID* column that you saw in the *Orders* table. If you scroll down to *VINET*, you can see that the company name of *VINET* is *Vins et alcools Chevalier*.

Notice that the *CustomerID* is unique for each record in the *Customers* table. In database terminology this is known as the *Primary Key* of the *Customers* table. Primary keys are used to uniquely identify each record in the table. Primary keys are usually named with the table name followed by *ID*, as you can see here.

Notice that the *CustomerID* is not unique in the *Orders* table. In database terminology it's known as a *Foreign Key*.

note

Database design errors

If you examine the database diagram on the next page you can see that the foreign key for the *ShipperID* is named *ShipVia* in the *Orders* table.

This is an example of a minor error in the database design, as primary and foreign keys should always have the same names. Without the database diagram it would be difficult to figure out that a relationship existed between the two tables.

Almost every real-world database contains errors of some kind. Working around these kind of issues is something you will have to do a lot as a database analyst.

The primary and foreign keys allow you to create a link (or *join*) between the two tables and write queries that extract data from two or more tables. In database terminology it can be said that there is a *relationship* between the tables.

You'll create your first query that extracts data from multiple tables in the next lesson: *Lesson 21: Use inner joins to extract data from multiple tables.*

4 Understand relationships.

Here is a diagram showing all of the relationships in the database.

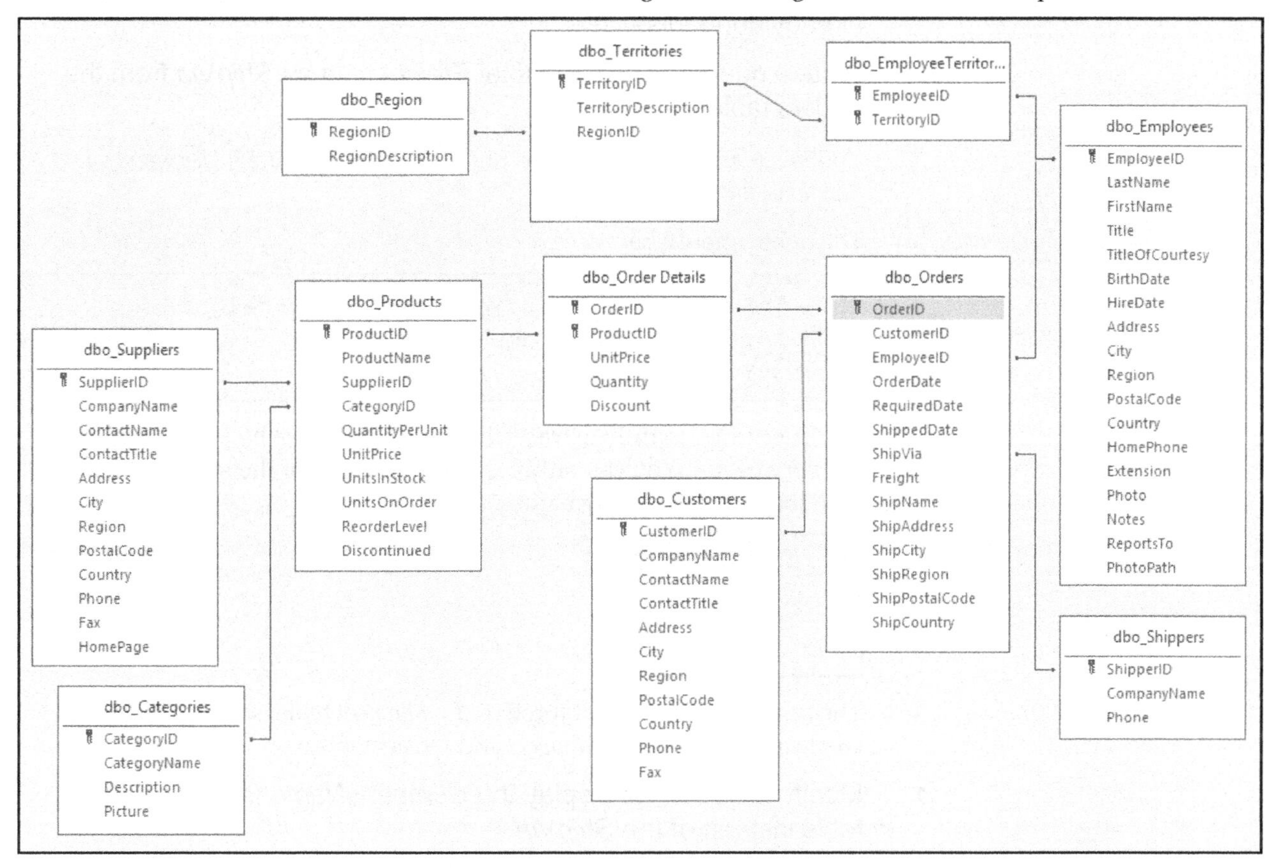

Database diagrams like this one are extremely useful to you as a database analyst. There are many different tools that can be used to create a database diagram, including SSMS itself. The database's administrator should be able to provide you with a database diagram for reporting purposes.

The lines on the diagram show relationships between primary and foreign keys. In the next lesson you'll learn how to create queries that use these relationships to extract data from multiple tables in a single query.

Lesson 21: Use inner joins to extract data from multiple tables

You learned about relationships in the previous lesson. You can exploit these to extract data from multiple tables by using *JOIN* commands in the *FROM* statement.

1 Open SSMS and connect to your SQL Server (if you haven't already done this).

2 Write a query to show the total *Freight* paid by *ShipVia* from the *Orders* table.

You've created similar queries previously, in: *Lesson 15: Use aggregate functions and GROUP BY.*

The query should be:

```
SELECT ShipVia, SUM(Freight) AS TotalFreight
FROM Northwind.dbo.Orders
GROUP BY ShipVia
```

The query successfully extracts the total freight cost by shipper, but it's not very useful. You can only see the ID number of the shippers rather than the actual company names.

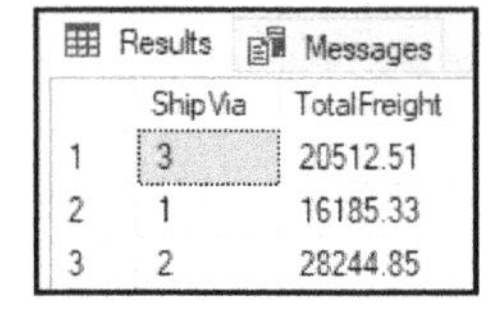

Results | Messages

	ShipVia	TotalFreight
1	3	20512.51
2	1	16185.33
3	2	28244.85

The company names are stored in the *Shippers* table, so you'll need to create a join to link the *Shippers* and *Orders* tables.

3 Modify the query to display the *CompanyName* from the *Shippers* table instead of the *ShipVia*.

1. Examine the database diagram.

   You can see the relationship that you need to use.

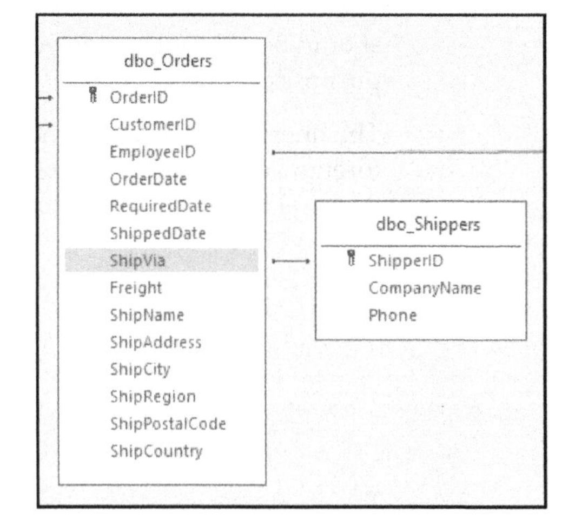

Primary keys and foreign keys typically have the same name. This is an exception (and an example of a database design error).

You can see that the *ShipperID* is the primary key and the *ShipVia* is the foreign key.

2. Modify the query as shown:

```
SELECT Shippers.CompanyName,
SUM(Orders.Freight) AS TotalFreight

FROM Northwind.dbo.Orders
INNER JOIN Northwind.dbo.Shippers ON Orders.ShipVia = Shippers.ShipperID

GROUP BY Shippers.CompanyName
```

Notice the new *INNER JOIN* command. Joins are always added as part of the *FROM* statement. This command tells the query to join the *Shippers* table to the *Orders* table by looking for records where *ShipVia* and *ShipperID* match.

You are now prefixing the column names with the table name to make it clear which table the column is from. This isn't strictly necessary unless the same column name could be found in both tables, but it's best practice and makes your queries more readable.

note

Inner joins are the default join type

There are multiple join types available in SQL Server.

The *inner* join is the default join type so you can actually perform an inner join by simply using the word *JOIN* alone.

It's better to use the complete join type to make it clearer which join type you are using.

3. Execute the query.

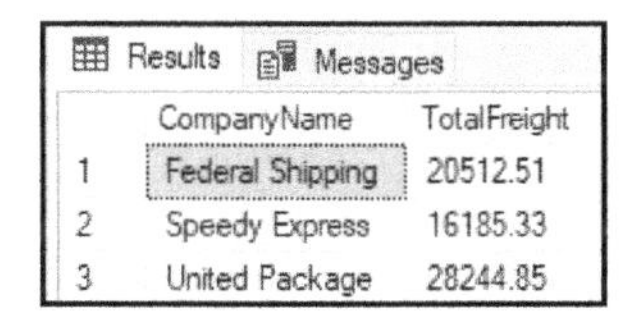

Results | Messages

	CompanyName	TotalFreight
1	Federal Shipping	20512.51
2	Speedy Express	16185.33
3	United Package	28244.85

You can now see the names of the 3 shipping companies, along with the amounts paid to each one.

Lesson 22: Use outer joins

There are several types of join available in SQL Server, but you'll use inner and outer joins more than any other kind. You'll see the difference between the two in this lesson.

1. Open SSMS and connect to your SQL Server (if you haven't already done this).

2. Write a query to show the total number of *Orders* made by each of the *Customers*.

   If you examine the database diagram you can see that you will need a join for this query.

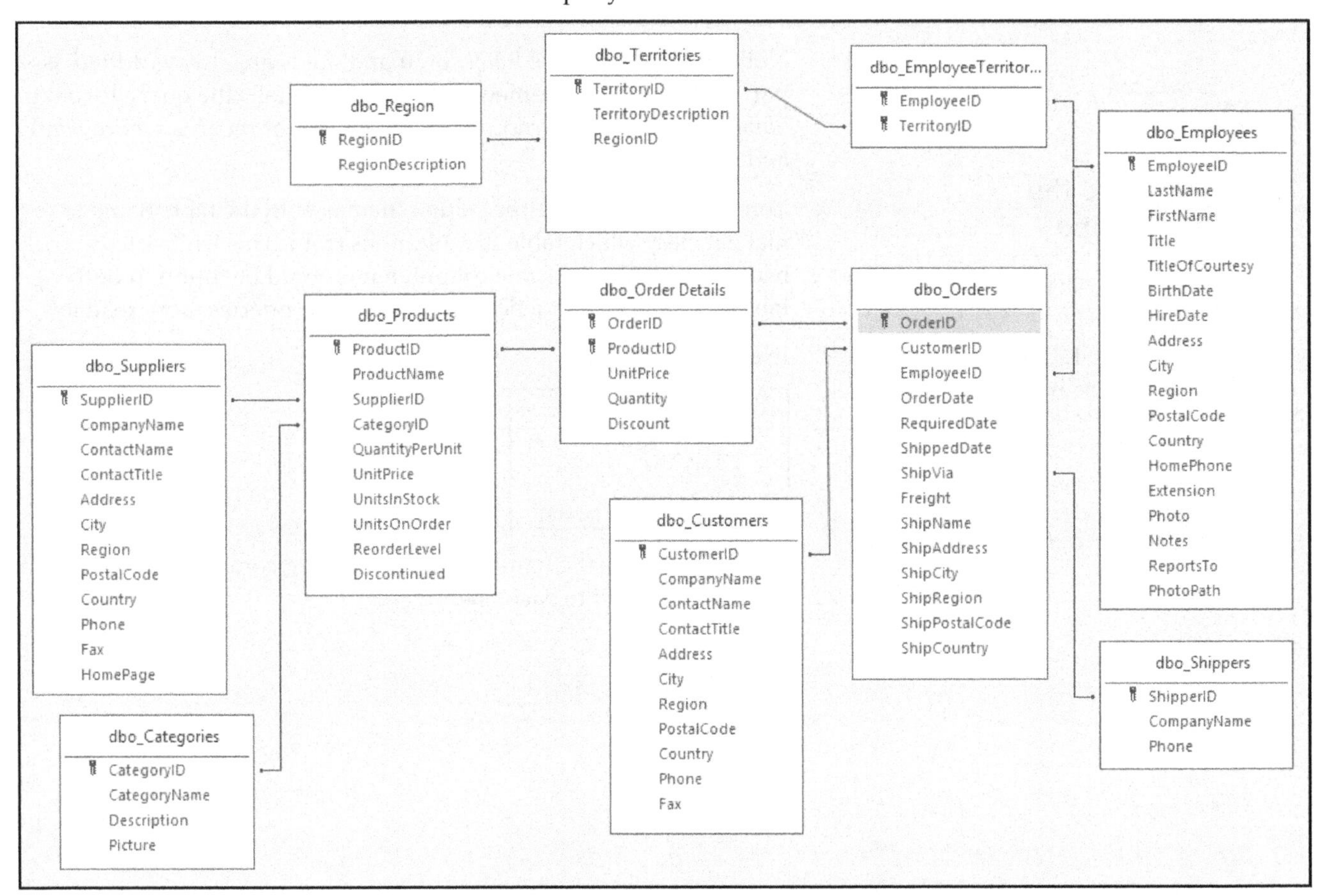

You'll need the *CompanyName* from the *Customers* table and the *OrderID* from the *Orders* table. You will need to join the two tables together along a relationship. If you look at the database diagram above, you can see that the two tables are linked by the *CustomerID*.

Once you have joined the tables together you will need to use the *COUNT* function to count the number of orders made by each customer. *COUNT* works just like the *SUM* function you learned about in: *Lesson 15: Use aggregate functions and GROUP BY*.

For brevity, this query isn't using the full *dbo.Northwind* qualifier that you've used in most previous queries. You'll need to make sure to select the *Northwind* database from the drop-down menu before running the queries. You saw how to do this in: *Lesson 5: Write your first database query*.

```
SELECT Customers.CompanyName,
COUNT(Orders.OrderID) AS TotalOrders
FROM Customers
INNER JOIN Orders ON Customers.CustomerID = Orders.CustomerID
GROUP BY Customers.CompanyName
ORDER BY COUNT(Orders.OrderID)
```

important

Outer joins are slower than inner joins

A database designer can include indexes in a database that speed up queries. For example, the records in the *Orders* table are indexed by the *CustomerID*, allowing the orders for each *Customer* to be extracted extremely quickly. When you use an *outer* join, the server needs to iterate through each individual record. This means it can't take advantage of indexes, often making your queries much slower.

You'll learn more about optimizing queries in: *Lesson 30: Analyze and optimize a query.*

The query extracts the total number of orders for each customer.

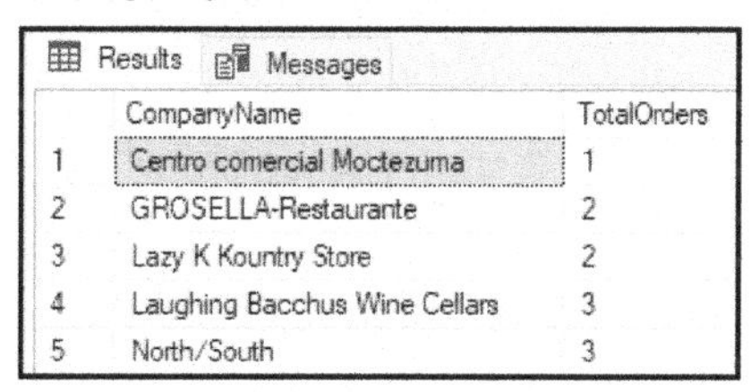

Results | Messages

	CompanyName	TotalOrders
1	Centro comercial Moctezuma	1
2	GROSELLA-Restaurante	2
3	Lazy K Kountry Store	2
4	Laughing Bacchus Wine Cellars	3
5	North/South	3

There are 91 customers in the *Customers* table, but this query is only showing 89 of them. That's because you are using an *INNER* join. Inner joins only display records when there is a matching record in both tables, so your query only shows customers that have placed at least one order. Customers that don't have any matching records in the *Orders* table are excluded from the query results.

This isn't always what you want. Sometimes you will want to see the customers that haven't placed orders as well. To display records from the *Customers* table even when there is no matching record in the *Orders* table you will need to use an *outer* join.

3 Modify the query to display all customers.

Modify the query as shown:

```
SELECT Customers.CompanyName,
COUNT(Orders.OrderID) AS TotalOrders
FROM Customers
LEFT JOIN Orders ON Customers.CustomerID = Orders.CustomerID
GROUP BY Customers.CompanyName
ORDER BY COUNT(Orders.OrderID)
```

note

Syntactic sugar

For improved readability, you can include the word *OUTER* after *LEFT* or *RIGHT*. For example:

```
LEFT OUTER JOIN
Orders
```

This is an example of 'syntactic sugar'. You don't need to include the word *OUTER*, but you can use it to make it clearer that you are using an outer join.

The results now include the two customers that do not have any orders.

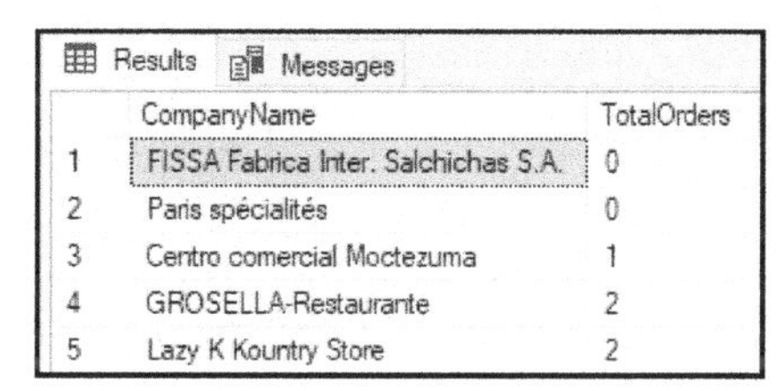

Results | Messages

	CompanyName	TotalOrders
1	FISSA Fabrica Inter. Salchichas S.A.	0
2	Paris spécialités	0
3	Centro comercial Moctezuma	1
4	GROSELLA-Restaurante	2
5	Lazy K Kountry Store	2

This is an example of a left *outer* join. It's called a left join because it returns all records from the leftmost table in the JOIN statement (the *Customers* table) and displays matching records from the rightmost table (*Orders*). It's important to enter the tables in the correct order when you are working with outer joins.

RIGHT JOIN is also supported by the SQL language, but it is usually better to use *LEFT JOIN* and make sure that the tables are entered in the correct order.

note

Natural joins

SQL Server offers a special join type called the *NATURAL* join.

The natural join type tries to make your job easier by automatically looking for matching column names and joining tables without needing to be told which columns match.

It's best to avoid using natural joins as they can make it unclear how tables are being joined. Natural joins are also not supported by many databases other than SQL Server.

Lesson 23: Use full joins

INNER and LEFT joins are by far the most common, but the FULL and CROSS join types enable you to carry out some more advanced joins.

You'll see how to use full joins in this lesson and cross joins in: *Lesson 24: Use cross joins.*

1. Open SSMS and connect to your SQL Server (if you haven't already done this).

2. Write a query to show which *Customers* are in the same country as their *Suppliers*.

   Ideally the database would have been designed with a *Country* table that would allow you to join *Customers* and *Suppliers* along a relationship, but there is no such relationship in this database.

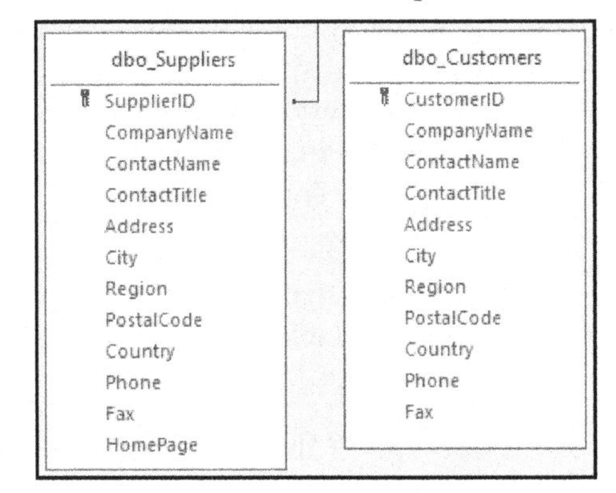

Even when there's no relationship you can still join tables together if they contain matching values. In this case you need to match the *Customers* and *Suppliers* based on the *Country* column that appears in both tables.

Execute the following query:

```
SELECT Suppliers.Country, Customers.Country,
Suppliers.CompanyName AS SupplierName,
Customers.CompanyName AS CustomerName
FROM Suppliers
INNER JOIN Customers ON Suppliers.Country = Customers.Country
ORDER BY Suppliers.Country, Customers.Country
```

The query results show, for example, that the company's supplier in Brazil is *Refrescos Americanas LTDA* and that there are 9 customers in the same country.

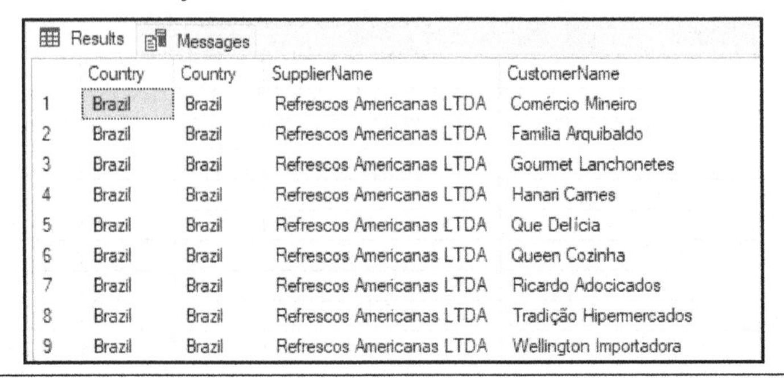

Results | Messages

	Country	Country	SupplierName	CustomerName
1	Brazil	Brazil	Refrescos Americanas LTDA	Comércio Mineiro
2	Brazil	Brazil	Refrescos Americanas LTDA	Familia Arquibaldo
3	Brazil	Brazil	Refrescos Americanas LTDA	Gourmet Lanchonetes
4	Brazil	Brazil	Refrescos Americanas LTDA	Hanari Carnes
5	Brazil	Brazil	Refrescos Americanas LTDA	Que Delícia
6	Brazil	Brazil	Refrescos Americanas LTDA	Queen Cozinha
7	Brazil	Brazil	Refrescos Americanas LTDA	Ricardo Adocicados
8	Brazil	Brazil	Refrescos Americanas LTDA	Tradição Hipermercados
9	Brazil	Brazil	Refrescos Americanas LTDA	Wellington Importadora

Since you've used an inner join, countries are only being displayed if they have both a supplier *and* a customer.

3 Modify the query to show all suppliers and customers.

You might be thinking you could use a left (or right) outer join. If you used a left join starting with the *Suppliers* table the query would return all customers that are in the same country as at least one supplier, but any customers that didn't have a supplier in their country would be excluded.

If you joined starting with the *Customers* table only suppliers that share a country with at least one customer would be displayed.

You need a join that displays all records from both tables: a *full* join. Full joins return all records from both sides of the join so it doesn't matter which order the tables are placed in the *JOIN* statement.

Modify the query to:

```
SELECT Suppliers.Country, Customers.Country, Suppliers.CompanyName
AS SupplierName,
Customers.CompanyName AS CustomerName
FROM Suppliers
FULL JOIN Customers ON Suppliers.Country = Customers.Country
ORDER BY Suppliers.Country, Customers.Country
```

When you execute the query the results now show all customers and suppliers.

You can see that there are 3 customers in Argentina, but no supplier in that country.

	Country	Country	SupplierName	CustomerName
1	NULL	Argentina	NULL	Cactus Comidas para llevar
2	NULL	Argentina	NULL	Océano Atlántico Ltda.
3	NULL	Argentina	NULL	Rancho grande

You can also see that there are two suppliers in Australia but no customers.

	Country	Country	SupplierName	CustomerName
23	Australia	NULL	Pavlova, Ltd.	NULL
24	Australia	NULL	G'day, Mate	NULL

The query results aren't as conveniently formatted as they could be. One of the two *Country* columns is *NULL* if there are no matching records in one of the tables.

You can clean up a query like this by using the *CASE* statement. You'll learn how to do this later in the course, in: *Lesson 25: Use the CASE* .

Lesson 24: Use cross joins

The *cross* join is the only major join type you haven't yet used. A cross join combines all records in both tables.

1 Open SSMS and connect to your SQL Server (if you haven't already done this).

2 Write a query to show the total units in stock held by each of the *Suppliers* by category.

If you examine the database diagram you can see that you will need two joins for this query.

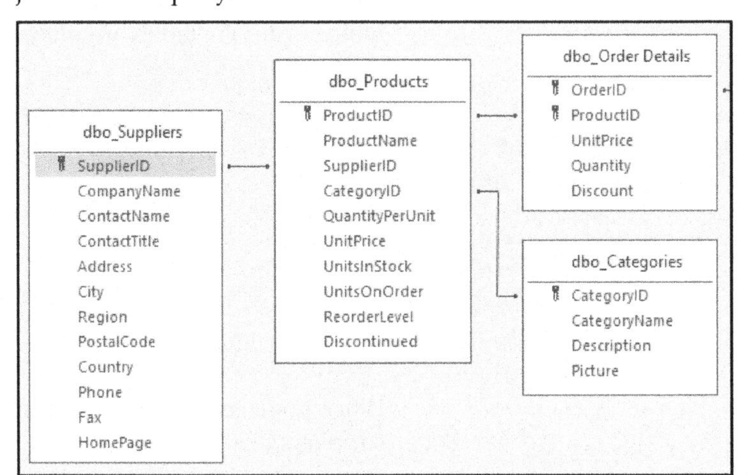

note

The ISNULL function

The ISNULL function allows you to specify a value that should be used instead of any NULL results. You can replace the NULL results of this query with zeroes by using:

```
ISNULL(SUM(
Products.UnitsInStock),0)
```

The supplier names are held in the *Suppliers* table. You'll need to join the *Products* table to get the units in stock. You'll also need to join the *Categories* table to get the category names.

Start by executing this query:

```
SELECT Suppliers.CompanyName, Categories.CategoryName,
SUM(Products.UnitsInStock)

FROM Products
INNER JOIN Suppliers ON Products.SupplierID = Suppliers.SupplierID
INNER JOIN Categories ON Products.CategoryID = Categories.CategoryID

GROUP BY Suppliers.CompanyName, Categories.CategoryName

ORDER BY Suppliers.CompanyName, Categories.CategoryName
```

This query uses two simple inner joins. You learned how to use these in: *Lesson 21: Use inner joins to extract data from multiple tables.*

You can also see that the query uses the *SUM* aggregate function and the *GROUP BY* statement that you learned how to use in: *Lesson 15: Use aggregate functions and GROUP BY*. The results show each supplier's units in stock by category, but categories that don't have any units in stock are not shown. This isn't always what you want.

	CompanyName	CategoryName	(No column name)
1	Aux joyeux ecclésiastiques	Beverages	86
2	Bigfoot Breweries	Beverages	183
3	Cooperativa de Quesos 'Las Cabras'	Dairy Products	108

3 Modify the query to show all categories for each supplier.

> **note**
>
> **Alternative syntax**
>
> You can also perform cross joins by simply separating table names with commas in the *FROM* statement.
>
> ```
> FROM Suppliers
> CROSS JOIN Categories
> ```
>
> ...is the same as:
>
> ```
> FROM Suppliers,
> Categories
> ```
>
> This won't work in conjunction with other join types, so it's usually best to use the full *CROSS JOIN* syntax.

This isn't as easy as it might at first seem. You might be thinking you could use *left* or *full* joins, but that approach will not work when joining 3 or more tables. To list every category for every supplier you will need to use a *cross* join.

1. Execute the following query:

```
SELECT Suppliers.CompanyName,
Categories.CategoryName
FROM Suppliers
CROSS JOIN Categories
ORDER BY Suppliers.CompanyName,
Categories.CategoryName
```

Notice that you don't need to specify any columns when using a cross join. Cross joins simply combine both tables; in this case it will show every record in the *Categories* table next to each record in the *Suppliers* table.

	CompanyName	CategoryName
1	Aux joyeux ecclésiastiques	Beverages
2	Aux joyeux ecclésiastiques	Condiments
3	Aux joyeux ecclésiastiques	Confections
4	Aux joyeux ecclésiastiques	Dairy Products
5	Aux joyeux ecclésiastiques	Grains/Cereals
6	Aux joyeux ecclésiastiques	Meat/Poultry
7	Aux joyeux ecclésiastiques	Produce
8	Aux joyeux ecclésiastiques	Seafood

All 8 categories are now shown for each supplier. Next you need to modify the query to extract the units in stock from the *Products* table.

2. Modify the query to:

```
SELECT Suppliers.CompanyName, Categories.CategoryName,
SUM(Products.UnitsInStock)
FROM Suppliers CROSS JOIN Categories
LEFT JOIN Products ON Suppliers.SupplierID = Products.SupplierID
AND Categories.CategoryID = Products.CategoryID
GROUP BY Suppliers.CompanyName, Categories.CategoryName
ORDER BY Suppliers.CompanyName, Categories.CategoryName
```

This is the first join you've used that has more than one join condition, allowing you to join the *Products* table on both the *SupplierID* and the *CategoryID*. Joins support the same logical operators as you used previously, in: *Lesson 14: Use logical operators and filter by date.*

The query shows all categories for all suppliers, showing *NULL* for categories that the supplier doesn't have units in stock for.

	CompanyName	CategoryName	(No column name)
1	Aux joyeux ecclésiastiques	Beverages	86
2	Aux joyeux ecclésiastiques	Condiments	NULL
3	Aux joyeux ecclésiastiques	Confections	NULL

note

Alternatives to CASE

If you're familiar with Microsoft Excel, you've probably encountered pivot tables that work similarly to this lesson's query.

As an alternative to CASE you could generate an Excel pivot table from the results of a much simpler query.

SQL Server also offers a special *PIVOT* statement, but it is not supported by other database products so it is best avoided unless your query will only be used on SQL Server databases.

Lesson 25: Use the CASE function

The *CASE* function allows you to perform logical operations upon the results of your queries. CASE has many uses, but it's most often used to group values together in custom columns.

1 Open SSMS and connect to your SQL Server (if you haven't already done this).

2 Write a query to show sales values by employee and country.

If you examine the database diagram you can see that the sales values can be calculated from the *Order Details* table, the employee details are in the *Employees* table and the *ShipCountry* is found in the *Orders* table.

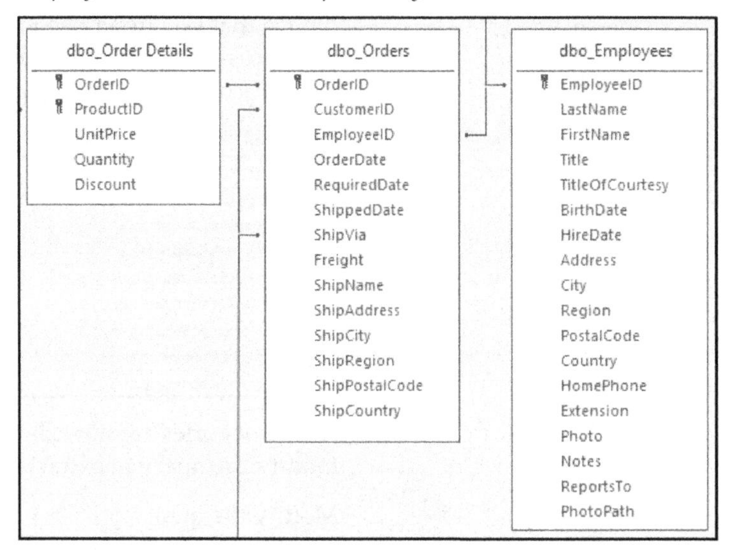

You should be able to extract the sales values by using the skills that you've already learned. You only need inner joins and the *SUM* function. The query should be:

```
SELECT Employees.FirstName + ' ' + Employees.LastName AS Employee,
Orders.ShipCountry,
SUM([Order Details].UnitPrice * [Order Details].Quantity) AS OrderValue

FROM Employees
INNER JOIN Orders ON Employees.EmployeeID = Orders.EmployeeID
INNER JOIN [Order Details] ON Orders.OrderID = [Order Details].OrderID

GROUP BY Employees.FirstName + ' ' + Employees.LastName, Orders.ShipCountry
ORDER BY Employees.FirstName + ' ' + Employees.LastName, Orders.ShipCountry
```

Notice that you're appending the *FirstName* and *LastName* columns as you did in: *Lesson 12: Concatenate text and numbers.*

You're multiplying the *UnitPrice* and *Quantity* to get the order value, just like you did in: *Lesson 11: Use simple mathematical operators and custom column names.*

3 Modify the query to split sales into UK, USA and Rest of World sales.

You already know how to filter the results by country, but you will need the CASE function to show different groupings within the same query.

The query you will need is:

```
SELECT Employees.FirstName + ' ' + Employees.LastName AS Employee,
SUM(CASE WHEN Orders.ShipCountry = 'UK'
    THEN [Order Details].UnitPrice * [Order Details].Quantity
    ELSE 0 END) AS UK,
SUM(CASE WHEN Orders.ShipCountry = 'USA'
    THEN [Order Details].UnitPrice * [Order Details].Quantity
    ELSE 0 END) AS USA,
SUM(CASE WHEN Orders.ShipCountry NOT IN ('UK','USA')
    THEN [Order Details].UnitPrice * [Order Details].Quantity
    ELSE 0 END) AS RestOfWorld
FROM Employees
INNER JOIN Orders ON Employees.EmployeeID = Orders.EmployeeID
INNER JOIN [Order Details] ON Orders.OrderID = [Order Details].OrderID
GROUP BY Employees.FirstName + ' ' + Employees.LastName
ORDER BY Employees.FirstName + ' ' + Employees.LastName
```

The *CASE* function allows you to impose logical constraints. Here's the *CASE* function to get the sales values for the *UK*:

```
SUM(CASE WHEN Orders.ShipCountry = 'UK'
    THEN [Order Details].UnitPrice * [Order Details].Quantity
    ELSE 0 END) AS UK
```

note

Nesting case functions

It's possible to nest multiple CASE functions inside one another by placing additional *CASE* functions after the *THEN* or *ELSE* keywords.

Nesting *CASE* functions can result in very complex queries that are difficult to understand, so it's usually best to avoid doing this.

If you do use nested *CASE* functions, remember that you can make your code more readable by using line breaks and tabs.

WHEN Orders.ShipCountry = 'UK' specifies that the statement should only apply to records where the *ShipCountry* is *UK*.

*THEN [Order Details].UnitPrice * [Order Details].Quantity* specifies that you want to multiply the *UnitPrice* and *Quantity* values for the *UK* records that were extracted.

ELSE 0 END specifies that a value of zero should be used for records that do not have the *ShipCountry* of *UK*.

The query results show the *UK, USA* and *RestOfWorld* sales for each employee.

	Employee	UK	USA	RestOfWorld
1	Andrew Fuller	3456.60	22780.60	151512.06
2	Anne Dodsworth	7070.30	18104.90	57788.80
3	Janet Leverling	4723.30	34809.23	173518.77
4	Laura Callahan	9334.20	27619.17	96347.66
5	Margaret Peacock	8871.11	50657.94	190658.40
6	Michael Suyama	4539.50	18711.69	54946.91
7	Nancy Davolio	11323.45	46382.60	144437.66
8	Robert King	6013.65	28349.75	106932.59
9	Steven Buchanan	5284.40	16151.10	54132.25

Lesson 26: Work with subqueries

So far you have always worked with one query at a time, but it's possible to create a query that works from the results of another query. This is known as a subquery or virtual table.

note

Alternatives to subqueries

It's possible to save a query onto the server as a *View*. Views can then be joined onto your queries just like ordinary tables.

Views can be cached and indexed by SQL Server, which makes them faster and more efficient than subqueries. It's best to use views instead of subqueries when a query needs to be reused.

You'll learn how to create views later in this course, in: *Lesson 29: Create a View*.

1 Open SSMS and connect to your SQL Server (if you haven't already done this).

2 Write a query to calculate the average sales made by employee in 1997.

Subqueries are often used in situations where you need to compare the records in a table with another value from within the same table.

In this case you will first need to calculate the sales that each employee made in 1997. You'll then need to use these values to calculate an average across all employees.

1. Execute the following query to calculate the total sales by employee in 1997.

```
SELECT Employees.EmployeeID,
SUM([Order Details].UnitPrice * [Order Details].Quantity) AS TotalSales

FROM Employees
INNER JOIN Orders ON Employees.EmployeeID = Orders.EmployeeID
INNER JOIN [Order Details] ON Orders.OrderID = [Order Details].OrderID

WHERE Orders.OrderDate >= '01 Jan 1997'
AND Orders.OrderDate < ='01 Jan 1998'

GROUP BY Employees.EmployeeID
```

The query extracts the total sales each employee made in 1997.

	EmployeeID	TotalSales
1	9	29577.55
2	3	111788.61
3	6	45992.00
4	7	66829.14
5	1	97533.58
6	4	139477.70
7	5	32595.05
8	2	76805.60
9	8	59776.52

You now need to calculate the average based upon these numbers. To do this you'll need to create a query that works upon the results of this query; in SQL terminology, you need to use this query as a *subquery*.

2. Modify the query to:

```
SELECT *
FROM (
      SELECT Employees.EmployeeID,
      SUM([Order Details].UnitPrice * [Order Details].Quantity) AS TotalSales
      FROM Employees
      INNER JOIN Orders ON Employees.EmployeeID = Orders.EmployeeID
      INNER JOIN [Order Details] ON Orders.OrderID = [Order Details].OrderID
      WHERE Orders.OrderDate >= '01 Jan 1997'
      AND Orders.OrderDate < ='01 Jan 1998'
      GROUP BY Employees.EmployeeID
) Subquery
```

As you can see, you've moved the query into the *FROM* statement. The results of the query will now be used in exactly the same way as any other table placed in the *FROM* statement would be. You can even join additional tables onto the subquery.

Notice the word *Subquery* after the brackets surrounding the subquery. This is the name that will be used to represent the subquery. You can set this to anything appropriate.

At the moment all you are asking the query to do is to extract all records from the subquery, so the results will be exactly the same as running the subquery on its own.

	EmployeeID	TotalSales
1	9	29577.55
2	3	111788.61
3	6	45992.00
4	7	66829.14
5	1	97533.58
6	4	139477.70
7	5	32595.05
8	2	76805.60
9	8	59776.52

3. Modify the query to:

```
SELECT AVG(Subquery.TotalSales) AS AverageSales
FROM (
      SELECT Employees.EmployeeID,
      SUM([Order Details].UnitPrice * [Order Details].Quantity) AS TotalSales
      FROM Employees
      INNER JOIN Orders ON Employees.EmployeeID = Orders.EmployeeID
      INNER JOIN [Order Details] ON Orders.OrderID = [Order Details].OrderID
      WHERE Orders.OrderDate >= '01 Jan 1997'
      AND Orders.OrderDate < ='01 Jan 1998'
      GROUP BY Employees.EmployeeID
) Subquery
```

The query now calculates the average sales per employee based on the subquery.

	AverageSales
1	73375.0833

Lesson 27: Use IN and EXISTS

You've worked with the IN keyword previously, in *Lesson 16: Work with NULL values and the IN keyword*. You'll see how to use IN with subqueries in this lesson, and how to use the EXISTS keyword to check if a subquery returns any records.

1 Open SSMS and connect to your SQL Server (if you haven't already done this).

2 Write a query to extract the names of all *Employees* that have made at least one sale to the UK.

1. Execute the following query to extract the *EmployeeID* values for all UK orders:

```
SELECT EmployeeID
FROM Orders
WHERE Orders.ShipCountry = 'UK'
```

You can now see the *EmployeeID* values for each UK order. Notice that there are duplicate records in the query results because you are seeing separate records for every UK order in the table.

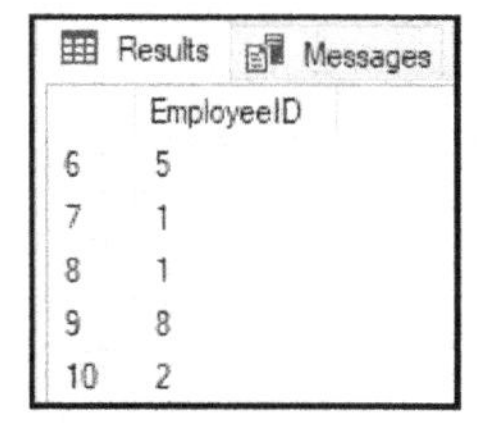

	EmployeeID
6	5
7	1
8	1
9	8
10	2

There are multiple ways to get a unique list of employee names from this data. You'll see three different solutions in this lesson.

2. Modify the query to:

```
SELECT Employees.FirstName, Employees.LastName
FROM Employees
WHERE
Employees.EmployeeID IN (
    SELECT EmployeeID
    FROM Orders
    WHERE Orders.ShipCountry = 'UK'
)
```

The IN keyword here returns records where the *EmployeeID* is found within the list of *EmployeeID* values returned by your subquery.

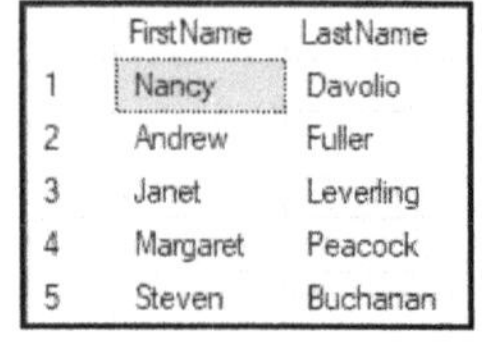

	FirstName	LastName
1	Nancy	Davolio
2	Andrew	Fuller
3	Janet	Leverling
4	Margaret	Peacock
5	Steven	Buchanan

3 Modify the query to use the *EXISTS* keyword instead of *IN*.

The query currently looks for *EmployeeID* values that are *IN* the list of *EmployeeID* values on UK orders. You could rephrase this and say that you want to see employees where a record *EXISTS* in the *Orders* table that has a *UK* country and a matching *EmployeeID*.

Modify the query to:

```
SELECT Employees.FirstName, Employees.LastName
FROM Employees
WHERE
EXISTS (
    SELECT EmployeeID
    FROM Orders
    WHERE Orders.EmployeeID = Employees.EmployeeID
    AND Orders.ShipCountry = 'UK'
)
```

The query results are exactly the same as with the previous query.

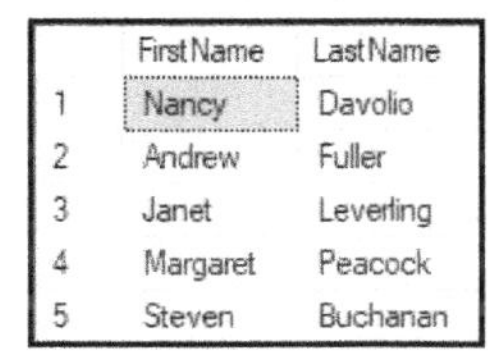

	FirstName	LastName
1	Nancy	Davolio
2	Andrew	Fuller
3	Janet	Leverling
4	Margaret	Peacock
5	Steven	Buchanan

Notice that you are referring to the *Employees.EmployeeID* from the 'parent' query within the subquery. This works, but it can quickly become confusing in more complex queries.

4 Modify the query to use ordinary joins instead of using a subquery.

There's one more way to get the same query results. Modify the query to:

```
SELECT DISTINCT Employees.FirstName, Employees.LastName
FROM Employees
INNER JOIN Orders ON Employees.EmployeeID = Orders.EmployeeID
WHERE Orders.ShipCountry = 'UK'
```

This solution doesn't use a subquery and extracts the same results.

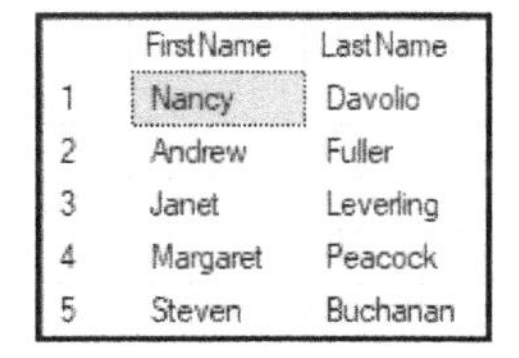

	FirstName	LastName
1	Nancy	Davolio
2	Andrew	Fuller
3	Janet	Leverling
4	Margaret	Peacock
5	Steven	Buchanan

This is actually the most efficient query to get the results you need. You'll see how to prove this in: *Lesson 30: Analyze and optimize a query.*

It's usually better to use ordinary joins if possible, but subqueries can be very useful with unusual queries, such as queries that extract data from more than one database.

Lesson 28: Use UNION to append the results of multiple queries together

Sometimes you need to run several different queries and return the results of all of them as a single table. The UNION keyword allows you to do this.

1 Open SSMS and connect to your SQL Server (if you haven't already done this).

2 Write queries to display the *City* values from the *Customers, Employees* and *Suppliers* tables.

Imagine that you want to create a complete list of cities where your company does business. There's no central *City* table in the database so you'll need to extract all of the cities that have been recorded in any of the database's tables.

Execute the following queries:

```
SELECT City
FROM Customers

SELECT City
FROM Employees

SELECT City
FROM Suppliers
```

You can enter all of these queries into the same query editor window in SSMS. When you execute the queries, you can see three different tables in the *Results* pane.

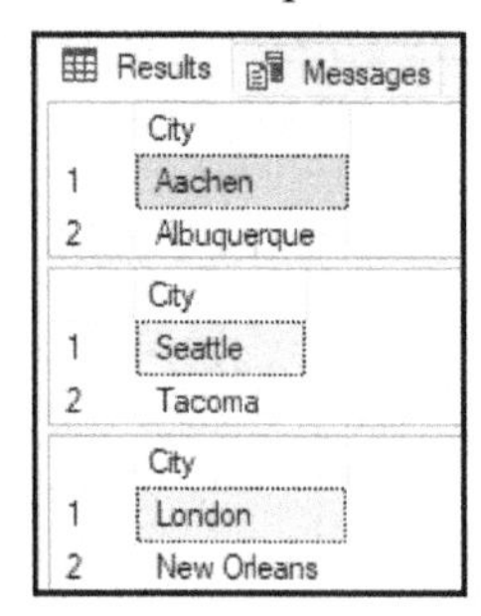

Notice that some of the city names are duplicated. For example, *London* appears in all 3 tables of results.

You can combine these queries into a single table by using the *UNION* keyword.

3 Combine the queries into a single table.

Modify the query to:

```
SELECT City
FROM Customers
UNION
SELECT City
FROM Employees
UNION
SELECT City
FROM Suppliers
ORDER BY City
```

The *UNION* keyword appends the results of two or more queries together into a single table.

UNION only returns unique records by default. If you wanted all of the duplicate records to be displayed as well, you could use *UNION ALL.*

Notice that there is only one *ORDER BY* statement. When you use *UNION, ORDER BY* sorts the final table after all queries have been appended. You can only use a single *ORDER BY* statement when you are using *UNION.*

When you execute the query a unique list of all cities is displayed.

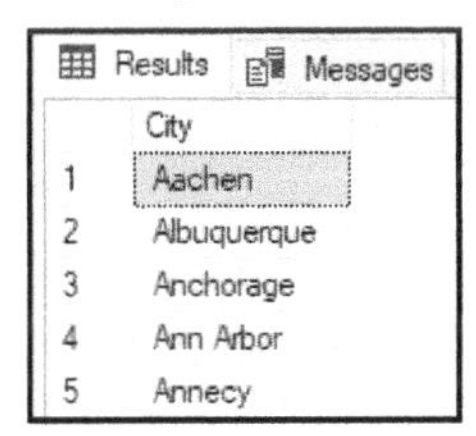

Lesson 29: Create a View

Views are queries that are saved onto the database server. A view can be used just like any other database table, making them extremely useful for simplifying your queries and speeding up your work.

1. Open SSMS and connect to your SQL Server (if you haven't already done this).

2. Create a View that shows total sales value by *Employee*.

   1. Expand the *Northwind* database in the *Object Explorer* pane.

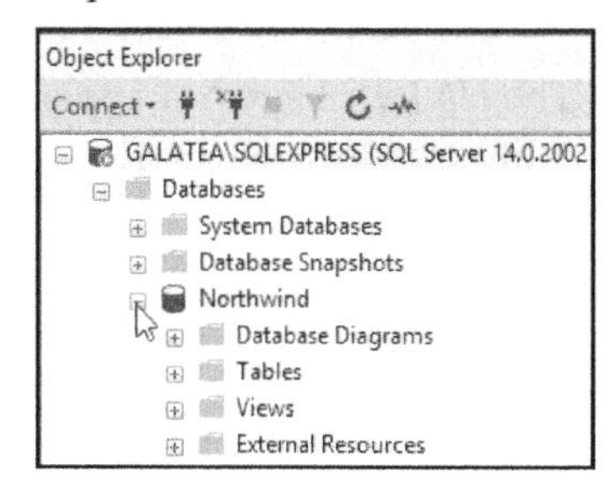

   Notice the *Views* folder inside the *Northwind* database.

   2. Expand the *Views* folder.

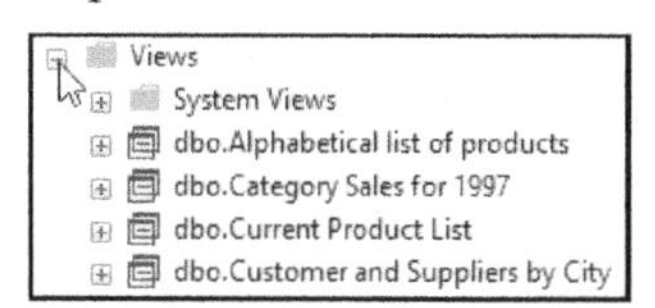

   You can see that several views already exist in the *Northwind* database.

   3. Right click on the *Views* folder and click *New View* from the shortcut menu.

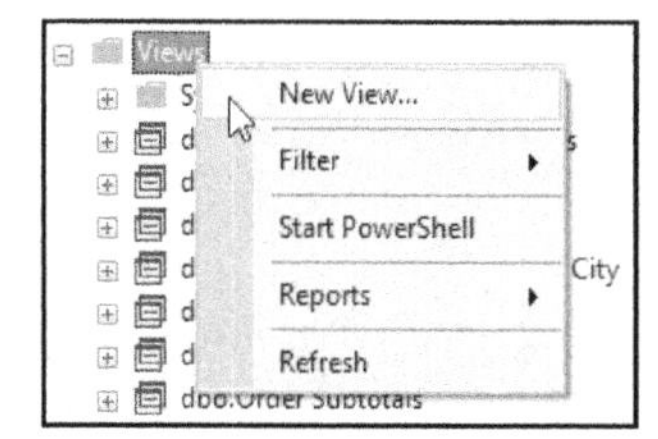

   A new view is created, and a dialog appears that asks you to choose tables to add to the view designer. The view designer is intended for users who don't understand the SQL language and is generally best avoided by users who are competent with SQL.

   4. Click the *Close* button to close the *Add Table* dialog.

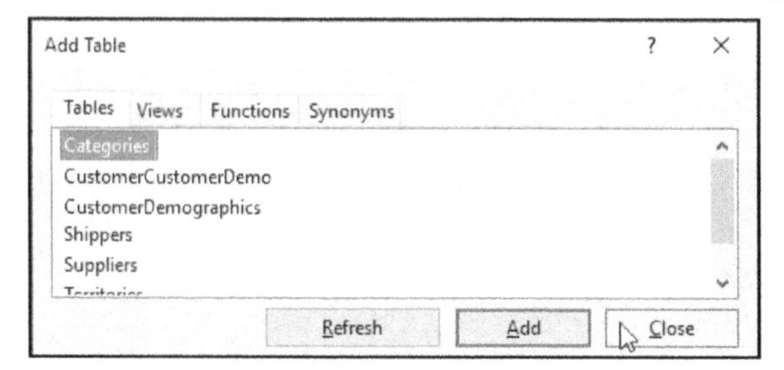

note

Database analysts often don't have permission to create views

In order to create a view your user account must have permission to do so. Most database analysts only have permission to view records from the database and aren't able to create views.

You should have full administrator's rights to the Northwind database, but in corporate systems you may need to ask the database administrator to create views for you if you're unable to get access rights to create them yourself.

note

Views, Stored Procedures and Functions

SQL Server allows queries to be saved as Views, Stored Procedures and Functions. You can see how to use Views in this lesson.

Stored Procedures are very similar to views and can even be used for the same purpose, but they are intended to be used to execute commands that insert, update or delete data so they are usually created by a database administrator.

SQL Server also allows you to create custom Functions that work in the same way as the functions you've used earlier in this course. These are also usually created by the database administrator.

5. Click in the pane at the bottom of the screen that currently contains *SELECT FROM*.

   This is the area where the view's SQL code resides.

6. Enter the following query:

```
SELECT Employees.EmployeeID,
SUM([Order Details].UnitPrice * [Order Details].Quantity) AS TotalSales

FROM Employees
INNER JOIN Orders ON Employees.EmployeeID = Orders.EmployeeID
INNER JOIN [Order Details] ON Orders.OrderID = [Order Details].OrderID

WHERE Orders.OrderDate >= '01 Jan 1997'
AND Orders.OrderDate < ='01 Jan 1998'

GROUP BY Employees.EmployeeID
```

   This is the query that you used as a subquery in *Lesson 26: Work with subqueries*. By saving it as a View you will be able to significantly simplify your queries.

7. Click: *File→Save [YOUR DATABASE].Northwind – dbo.View1.*

   You are prompted to provide a name for the new view.

8. Name the view: **VWSalesByEmployee** and click *OK*.

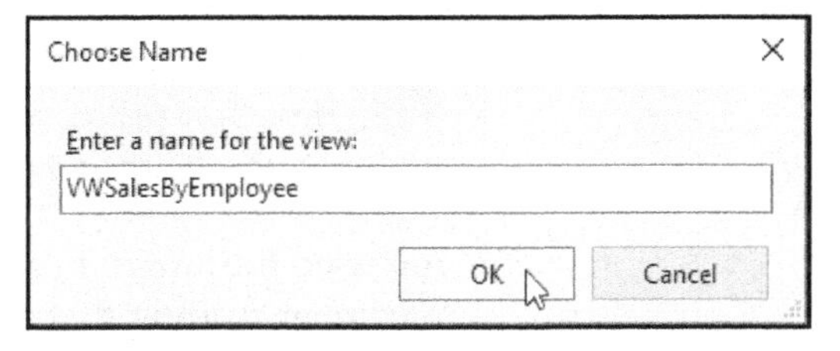

   The view is saved.

note

Naming views

You'll notice that you named your view with a prefix of *VW*. This makes it clear that your query is using a View rather than an ordinary table.

There's no consensus on the correct way to name Views, tables and other objects in databases so you may find that different naming conventions are used in different databases that you work with.

It's most important to be consistent with your names, regardless of which naming convention you use.

3 Create a query that uses your new view to get the average sales by employee.

This is the same task that you performed using a subquery in *Lesson 26: Work with subqueries*. Now that the sales data is available as a View you can extract the average sales with a much simpler query.

1. Create a new query window.
2. Execute the following query:

```
SELECT AVG(TotalSales)
FROM VWSalesByEmployee
```

   The average sales are extracted without needing a complex subquery.

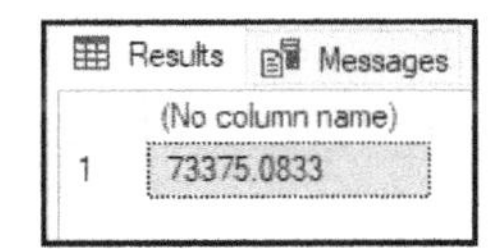

Lesson 30: Analyze and optimize a query

For one-off queries you rarely need to worry about how efficiently the query runs. The only exception is with very large databases or complex queries that may take a long time to run.

Some queries are used over and over again, especially if they are used by computer programs or websites. These queries may have to run hundreds of times per minute, and even a very small optimization could make a big difference.

SSMS includes tools that enable you to analyze your queries and ensure that they work in the best possible way.

1 Open SSMS and connect to your SQL Server (if you haven't already done this).

2 Compare two ways of extracting records for 1997.

1. Enter the following query:

```
SELECT OrderID,
YEAR(OrderDate) AS Year,
MONTH(OrderDate) AS Month,
DAY(OrderDate) AS Day
FROM Northwind.dbo.Orders
WHERE YEAR(OrderDate)=1997
```

You used this query in *Lesson 18: Use date functions*. You might remember reading that it isn't the most efficient way to query by date.

2. Click: *Query→Include Live Query Statistics.*

With this setting enabled, SSMS will gather statistics about the query as it runs and display them after the query is complete.

You can also enable and disable this feature by using the icon on the top toolbar.

3. Execute the query.

The query executes and the *Live Query Statistics* pane is displayed at the bottom of the screen.

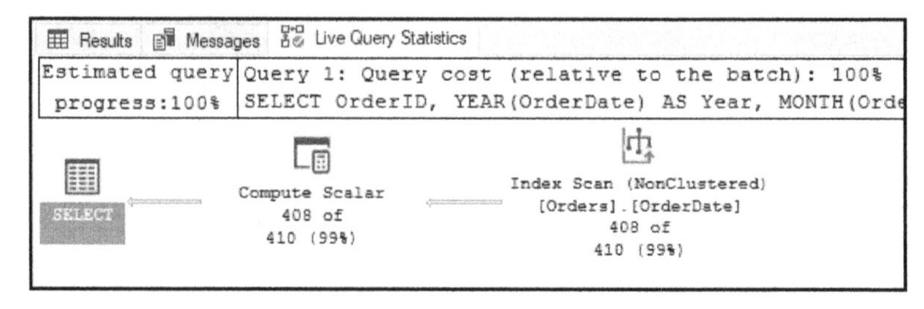

Notice that you can switch back to viewing the query results by clicking the *Results* tab.

note

Displaying an execution plan without running the query

When working with very large databases or very complex queries it may take a long time for a query to run, or you may want to avoid putting unnecessary load on the database server.

SSMS can generate an estimate of the steps a query will need without actually executing the query.

To generate an estimated execution plan, click: *Query→Display Estimated Execution Plan.*

You can also do this by clicking the icon on the top toolbar.

note

A database administrator can help to improve query performance

The performance of your queries isn't only down to the SQL code you use. The indexes that the database designer has applied to the database can massively improve query performance.

When you see *Scan* rather than *Seek* in the query statistics it's usually possible to speed up the query by adding an index to the database.

Indexes can be created by the database administrator, so you will need to work together with them to speed up your queries with indexes.

The statistics are a little cryptic. The three icons represent 3 operations that the database had to carry out to retrieve your results. If you look at the arrows you can see that they were executed from right to left.

Index Scan (NonClustered) [Orders].[OrderDate] means that the database looked through the *Orders* table to find the records where the year was 1997.

The word *Scan* is the most important part here. An *Index Scan* looks through each individual record in the table one by one and can be very slow with large tables.

The *Computer Scalar* operation represents the YEAR, MONTH and DAY functions in the SELECT statement. You will see this whenever you use aggregate functions.

4. Modify the query to:

```
SELECT OrderID,
YEAR(OrderDate) AS Year,
MONTH(OrderDate) AS Month,
DAY(OrderDate) AS Day
FROM Northwind.dbo.Orders
WHERE OrderDate >= '01 Jan 1997'
AND OrderDate < '01 Jan 1998'
```

This query avoids using the YEAR function in the WHERE statement.

5. Execute the query and examine the query statistics.

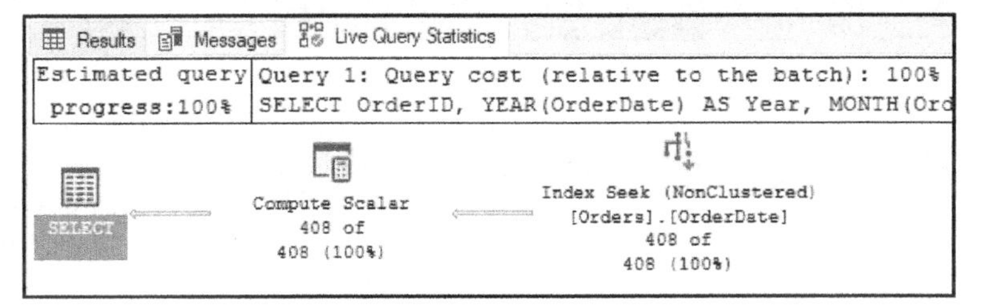

This time you can see that the query used an *Index Seek* instead of an *Index Scan*. This means that the query was able to make use of an index that was included by the database's designer.

Indexes automatically create catalogs for records in a database, making them much quicker to query. In this case, the index on the *OrderDate* column will have already catalogued all of the records by year so the database doesn't need to iterate through every record in the table to find the ones for 1997.

Index seeks are much faster and more efficient. This proves that the second query is better than the first and that you should avoid using aggregate functions to filter dates.

You can see more in-depth information about each step of the query by hovering your mouse cursor over the icons, including exactly how long each operation took. You can use this information to isolate the reason why a query may run slowly.

Index

E

F

N

O

P

Q

R

S

T

U

V

W

X

Y

Made in the USA
Las Vegas, NV
31 August 2021